A COMMENTARY ON THE CHYMICAL WEDDING OF CHRISTIAN ROSENKREUTZ

GW00691980

A Commentary on the Chymical Wedding of Christian Rosenkreutz Anno 1459

Margaret Bennell and Isabel Wyatt

Originally published by The Michael Press
Hawkwood College, 1965

This edition © Temple Lodge Press 1989

Cover design by Paulo Frank Boer

British Library Cataloguing in Publication Data
Wyatt, Isabel
    A commentary on the chymical wedding
    of Christian Rosenkreutz.
    1. Rosicrucianism. Andreæ, Johann Valentin
    Chymical wedding of Christian Rosenkreutz.
    Critical studies
    I. Title   II. Bennell, Margaret
    135 ± .43

ISBN 0-90469-313-9

Typeset by Emset, London NW10 4EH
Printed by The Camelot Press Southampton

CONTENTS

FOREWORD

The Chymical Wedding of Christian Rosenkreutz: Anno 1459 was written down in 1604 and first published in Strasbourg in 1616, having been widely circulated in manuscript during the intervening years.

The author was Johann Valentin Andreæ, then a seventeen-year-old student in Tübingen University, later to become a Lutheran pastor. Of him Rudolf Steiner says: 'His hand wrote it, his body was present; but through him a spiritual power not then on earth wished to communicate this to men, in a way which at that time was possible.'[1]

Karl Heyer, in his lecture course on 'The Historical Impulse of Rosicrucianism', says: 'The year 1459 in the title indicates the year in which—in a decisive and actual way— the new Rosicrucian Movement was founded in the West.'[2]

In his lecture, 'European Mysteries and their Initiates', Rudolf Steiner speaks of Rosicrucianism as 'a Mystery School having as its aim the cultivation of an understanding of the Christ Mystery in a way suited to the new era.' It is a continuation of the Order of the Grail and the Order of the Templars; its contents are couched in different terms in succeeding centuries to meet changes in human consciousness and changing human needs.

When *The Chymical Wedding* was first written down, it was still possible to convey spiritual revelations as they are here conveyed, in pictorial imaginations. Later, such imaginations dried out into abstract, purely conceptual thinking. Today the time is ripe to enliven the intellectual consciousness into a renewed pictorial one. It is therefore in accordance with the spiritual demands of the moment that *The Chymical Wedding* again begins to attract notice and that its beautiful sequence of imaginative pictures again begin to speak to our hearts and understanding.

The Chymical Wedding tells of a spiritual adventure, a kind of initiation journey, undertaken by Christian

Rosenkreutz as the pioneer of a new way into higher worlds. It is therefore a significant book for our time, one that should be studied both for the deep impression made by its Mystery pictures and for an understanding of its spiritual revelations. We need it as a traveller needs a guide-book and map when he journeys into an unknown land, for the journey of which it tells is a journey we must all take sooner or later.

Who was, who is, Christian Rosenkreutz?[3]

Rudolf Steiner has told us that in the middle of the thirteenth century a child was born who had a very special destiny. He came into the care of the twelve wisest men of that age who by world destiny were gathered in a certain spot in Europe. The child was very carefully trained by them, and taught their twelve-fold wisdom. As a young man he became very ill; he took no nourishment; his body became almost transparent; and finally he lay in a trance for some days. When he returned to consciousness it seemed as if the twelve streams of wisdom had been woven by him into an all-embracing fabric. Soon after this he died, having in this incarnation been kept withdrawn from outer earthly activity. According to Steiner, he was reborn in 1378. In 1406, when he was twenty-eight years of age, he began a seven-year journey to many Centres of Wisdom, returning in 1413, when he was thirty-five years of age.[4]

He gathered from these Centres the essence of their teaching and now grasped intellectually the radiant wisdom that had suffused his feeling-life in the previous century. He was just over eighty years of age when the experience came to him which is recounted in *The Chymical Wedding*. At the age of 106 he died.[5]

This individuality is said to have reappeared at the French Court at the time of the French Revolution as the Comte de St Germain. He warned the royal family and the nobility of their approaching fate, but in vain. He gave to the world the watchwords 'Liberty, Equality, Fraternity'; and though these were misunderstood by the French Revolutionists in the first flush of wild excitement, rightly interpreted they can become watchwords of our present epoch and the key to the development of the future.[6]

It is said that Christian Rosenkreutz is in almost con-
tinuous incarnation powerfully directing events from a hidden Centre, and always in the service of the Christ Power.
Those who wish to know more of this important subject
should read *The Mission of Christian Rosenkreutz* by Rudolf
Steiner.

Plato said of the myth of Isis and Osiris that it could be
understood on twenty different levels, and was true on all
of them. This could equally be said of *The Chymical Wedding*. Our Commentary looks at its pictures on the very
simplest level; but for those who would go deeper a few
slight indications of further levels are given in the Notes.

This booklet is the substance of a course of lectures
originally given at Hawkwood College, 2 – 9 July 1964. It
is offered in the hope that it may be of some pleasure and
profit to those without as well as within the Anthroposophical Movement.

A distinguished Dutch lecturer who was present at the
Hawkwood Course wrote later: 'I have started to read *The
Chymical Wedding* and now I begin to love it. I can read
it ten times, like a child with its picture-book.' This accords
with Rudolf Steiner's indication that all imaginative
knowledge based on truth is healing and health-giving, and
that the best educator is this same imaginative knowledge,
an indication of which points to the importance of study-
ing such pictorial records of spiritual life as this story.

The outline of the story, which has been included for
readers not already familiar with the book itself, has of
necessity had to be reduced to barest essentials; but as far
as possible we have retained the phraseology of the first
translation into English (made by Foxcroft in 1690) since
this carries with it something of the flavour of the language
of the period in which it was first written.

Margaret Bennell
Isabel Wyatt
1965

Part One

Outline of the Story

The First Day

On Easter Eve I was sitting at my table in my cottage on a hilltop, preparing my heart for the next day's festival, when all of a sudden there arose so horrible a tempest that the hill whereon my little house was founded was like to fly all in pieces.

I feared this to be another trick of the devil, who had done me many a spite, and now I felt my coat being twitched behind me. Hugely terrified, I turned to look, and there I beheld a fair and glorious lady, in garments of sky-blue, bespangled with golden stars, and with large and beautiful wings, full of eyes, wherewith she could mount aloft and fly swifter than any eagle. In her right hand was a golden trumpet, and in her left a great bundle of letters in all languages, which she (as I afterwards understood) was to carry into all countries.

From among them she chose a small one and laid it reverently on the table. Then, without speaking, she spread her wings and mounted upwards, blowing so mighty a blast on her gallant trumpet that for a full quarter of an hour afterward the whole hill echoed thereof.

I took up the letter in fear and trembling, and found it so heavy as almost to outweigh gold. It was sealed with a little seal which bore a curious cross, together with the inscription, 'In this sign conquer', at which I felt greatly comforted, knowing that this sign was little acceptable, and much less useful, to the devil.

Inside I found this verse written, in golden letters on an azure ground:

> This day, this day, this, this,
> The Royal Wedding is.
> If you by birth and by God's choice
> Are bidden to this feast, rejoice!
> Forthwith now to the mountain wend
> Whereon three stately Temples stand,
> And there see all from end to end.
> Yourself examine first with care;

> Let him who weighs too light beware;
> No guest this Wedding can endure
> Who keeps not watch and is not pure.

As I read these warnings, all my hair stood on end. Seven years previously, I had learned in a vision that one day I would be invited to a Royal Wedding, and when I now calculated the positions of the planets, I found that this was indeed the appointed time. But when I examined myself, as bidden by the letter, and contemplated my blindness in mysterious things, my ticklings of the flesh, my rearing of stately palaces in the air and other like carnal designs, I was so overwhelmed by my own unworthiness that I swung between hope and fear. The obscure words concerning the three Temples also afflicted me. At last I begged of my good angel that I might be rightly directed in my sleep.

In my sleep I found myself in a dark dungeon, fettered, with a multitude of companions all struggling with their chains and swarming like bees over each other. When presently we heard trumpets and kettle drums, and the dungeon was uncovered and a small light lowered into it, I contrived to slip from under the rest and heave myself onto a boulder against the dungeon wall.

Then an old man with ice-grey locks appeared at the edge of the opening, calling for silence. He announced that, by the grace of his ancient Mother, a rope would be let down seven times among us, and that whoever was able to cling to it would be drawn up and set at liberty.

When the Ancient Matron's servants let down the rope, I could get nowhere near it, while the heaving of the rest was pitiful to see. After seven minutes a little bell rang, and the rope was drawn up with four men clinging to it. Again and yet again the rope descended, and each time a few more were drawn up, those already released helping the servants to pull.

At its sixth lowering, the rope swung aside, so that I was able to catch it, and so beyond all hope came out, bleeding from a head-wound received from a sharp stone on the way. Now the dungeon was covered again, and those of us who had been drawn up were freed from our fetters, and our names recorded on a golden tablet. As we thanked the Ancient Matron for our deliverance and took our leave of her, each of us was given a piece of gold to spend by the way, stamped on one side with the rising sun, and on the other with the letters D.L.S.

As for me, I could scarcely well go forward for the wounds left on my feet by the fetters. The Ancient Matron, seeing this, said to me: 'My son, let not this defect afflict you, but thank God, who hath permitted you, even in this world, to come into so high a light. Keep these wounds for my sake.'

Pondering my dream when I awoke, I well understood from it that God had vouchsafed me to be present at this mysterious and hidden Wedding. So I rose and arrayed myself in a white linen coat with a blood-red stole bound crosswise over my shoulders; then, with four red roses stuck in my hat, and taking bread, salt and water for food by the way, I set out joyfully on my journey.

The Second Day

Now I went singing through a forest filled with Nature's rejoicings, emerging on a green heath, where stood three tall cedar trees, to one of which was fastened a tablet, offering a choice of four ways to the Wedding.

The first it described as short but dangerous, leading into rocky places scarcely possible to pass. The second was long but easy, provided we kept to it and were guided by our magnet. The third was a royal road, which only one in a thousand might follow. The fourth was a consuming way, encompassed by fire and cloud, fit only for incorruptible bodies.

The tablet warned us that once we had entered upon any of these ways there could be no turning back, and that if we knew ourselves by the smallest fault to be unworthy, we should not venture further.

At these dire warnings, I sank down beneath the tree in great perturbation of spirit. While I sat perplexed, pondering whether to turn back and, if not, which way to follow,

I took out a slice of my bread from my bag and began to eat.

At once a snow-white dove fluttered down from the branches above, betaking herself to me very familiarly, and I willingly shared my slice of bread with her. But now a black raven darted down at the dove, who took refuge in flight, the raven hastening after her and I after him.

When I had chased the raven away, I bethought me of my bag and bread, left behind beneath the cedar. But when I turned myself about, to go back to retrieve them, a contrary wind was so strong against me that it was ready to fell me; yet if I went forward, I perceived no hindrance. Looking about me, I saw I was already, without my knowledge, entered upon one of the four ways—the long, circuitous one.

So all that day I followed this road, taking care to stray neither to the left nor to the right. The way itself was so rugged that I was often in doubt about it; but the dove had flown due south, so with the help of my compass I kept strictly to that direction.

At last, just as the sun was setting, I spied a stately Portal, set high on a distant hill. So now I made mighty haste to reach it before nightfall, seeing elsewhere no other abiding-place.

As I drew near, a venerable man in a sky-blue habit stepped forth, made himself known as the Guardian of the Portal, and asked for my Letter of Invitation. With what joy did I present it!

When the Guardian heard my name and that I was a Brother of the Rose Cross, he both wondered and seemed to rejoice at it, and treated me with abundance of respect, saying: 'Come in, my brother. An acceptable guest you are to me!' In exchange for my bottle of water, the Guardian gave me a golden token, and with it a sealed letter for the Guardian of the Second Portal, entreating me that when these stood me in good stead I would remember him.

Dusk was now falling, and a beautiful Virgin, robed in sky-blue and bearing a glorious torch, was lighting lanterns along the road to the inner Portal. To this I hastened, and was dismayed to find it barred by a terrible chained lion who, as soon as he espied me, arose and made at me with great roaring.

This awoke the Guardian who was asleep on a slab of marble; he drove back the lion and, having read the sealed letter, greeted me with great respect, crying: 'Now welcome in God's name unto me, the man who of long time I would gladly have seen!' In exchange for my salt, this second Guardian gave me a second token.

By now the dusk had deepened, and a bell began to ring within the Castle. The Guardian warned me to run apace, or I would not reach the innermost gate before it closed for the night. The lights along the path were already being extinguished, and I was thankful to have the Virgin's torch to guide me through the darkness. As I entered the Third Portal at her very heels, the gate clapped to so suddenly that part of my coat was locked out and, since its Guardian could not be prevailed upon to open the gate again, had to be left behind.

The third Guardian now wrote my name in a little book of vellum, and gave me a third token, together with a new pair of shoes, for the floor of the Castle was pure shining marble. My old pair I bestowed on a beggar who sat by the gate.

Two pages, each bearing a torch, now conducted me into the Castle, and left me alone in a little room where, to my terror, invisible barbers cut away the hair from the crown of my head, but on my forehead, ears and eyes they permitted my ice-grey locks to hang. The hair cut off was carefully gathered up by invisible hands and carried away.

Now a little bell began to ring and the two pages, returning, lighted me through many doors and up winding stairs to a spacious hall where there was a great multitude of guests—emperors, kings, princes, lords, noble and ignoble, rich and poor, all sorts of people, including some I knew well, and as yet had never any reason to esteem; these, when I enquired of them as to their route, I found had mostly been forced to clamber over the rocks.

When, presently, trumpets sounded to bid us to the feast, these were they who scrambled for the highest seats, so that for me and some other sorry fellows there was hardly a little nook left at the lowermost table. But next to me was sitting a very fine, quiet man, who discoursed of excellent matters.

Meat was now brought in and served by invisible hands, everything so orderly managed that it seemed as if every guest had his own attendant. When one boasted that he could see these invisible servitors, one of them reached him so handsome a cuff upon his lying muzzle that not only he, but many who were by him, became mute as mice.

As they grew warm with wine, these guests of the lewder sort began to vaunt of their abilities; one heard the movements of the Heavens, the second could see Plato's Ideas, the third could number the atoms of Democritus. One would prove this, another that; and commonly the most sorry idiots made the loudest noise.

In this tumult I had almost cursed the day wherein I had come hither, and I opined that the Lord Bridegroom would have done well to seek some other fool than me for his wedding. But this was really one part of the lameness whereof I had dreamed.

Suddenly we heard strains of such delicate music that the babel was hushed and no one spoke one word for the space of half an hour. Then came louder music, all so master-like as if the Emperor of Rome had been entering. The door opened of itself, and many thousands of lighted tapers entered marching of themselves, and followed by a gliding gilded throne, on which sat the Virgin whose torch had lighted me to the Castle. She was robed no longer in sky-blue, but in snow-white, sparkling with purest gold. She welcomed us in the name of the Bride and the Bridegroom, but warned us that next morning we must all be weighed, to determine which were worthy to stay and assist at the Wedding. Any who felt assured of his own worthiness was now to be conducted to his bed chamber; any who felt doubtful was to spend the night in this hall.

When she had departed on her gliding throne, the tapers, held by invisible hands, conducted the confident to their beds. Only I and eight others remained in the hall, among them my table companion. An hour later, pages came in, bound all nine of us with ropes, and left us to spend the night in darkness and discomfort, bewailing our presumption in accepting the Wedding invitation.

But during the night I dreamed that I stood on a high

mountain, overlooking a great valley, in which a multitude
of men were suspended, some high, some low, by ropes
looped round their necks. An ancient man flew up and down
among them, cutting the ropes with his shears. Those who
had hung near the earth fell gently; those who had hung
high had a most shameful fall. This scene joyed me at the
heart till, in my highest fit of jollity, I waked.

This dream I recounted to my companion who felt
assured that by it some comfort was intended. So he and
I lay side by side in the dark, and passed the time till
daybreak in harmonious discourse.

The Third Day

At daybreak those who had deemed themselves worthy
came again into the hall where we others still lay bound.
Then a fanfare of trumpets ushered in the Virgin, arrayed
now in red velvet girded with a white scarf, and on her head
a green wreath of laurel, which much became her.

She was attended by two hundred knights in armour, with
surcoats of red and white; some of these she directed to
unbind us, and to place us where we could see well what
was to follow. Seeing me among them, she laughed and
exclaimed: 'Good lack! Have you also submitted yourself
to the yoke? I imagined you would have made yourself very
snug!'

Great golden scales were now brought in and hung in the
middle of the hall; beside them was placed a little table
covered with red velvet and bearing seven weights—a pretty
great one, then four little ones, then two great ones
severally; these weights in proportion to their bulk were
so heavy that no man can believe it. The knights were
divided into seven groups, the captain of each being placed
in charge of one of the weights.

A stately Emperor was the first to step into the scale. One
by one the captains laid in their weights; the first six he
withstood, but when the seventh was added he was
outweighed; he was therefore bound and delivered over in
great anguish to the sixth band of knights. One by one the

other Emperors were in turn weighed and also found wanting, except the last, who held out so steadfastly that
methought had there been more weights he would have
outstood these too.

To him the Virgin, rising and bowing, gave a red velvet
gown and a laurel branch, and seated him on the steps of
her throne.

The other ranks—kings, lords, gentry, learned and
unlearned—were now all weighed in turn. In each condition, one at most two, but mostly none, passed the test;
those who did so were, like the Emperor, honoured with
a red velvet gown, a laurel bough, and a seat on the steps
of the Virgin's throne.

Now it was our turn, we who had slept in the hall. Only
my companion and I outstayed all the weights. My companion held out bravely, whereupon all applauded him, and
the Virgin showed him deep respect. When, with trembling,
I myself stepped up, my companion, who already sat by
in his velvet, looked friendly upon me, and the Virgin herself
smiled a little.

So far did I outstay all the weights that to these the Virgin
added three knights in full armour. Still I outweighed them
all, upon which one of the pages stood up, and cried out
exceeding loud: 'This is he!' Because I had proved the
weightiest, the Virgin graciously permitted me to release
one of the captives, whomsoever I pleased. I elected the
first Emperor, who was immediately set free, and with all
respect seated among us. Meanwhile the Virgin espied my
roses, which I had taken out of my hat into my hands;
thereupon by her page she graciously requested them of me,
which I readily sent her.

By ten in the forenoon we had all been weighed. At the
meal which followed, we in our red velvet robes were
seated at the high table, which was also decked with red
velvet and set with drinking-cups of pure silver and gold.
Here two pages presented to us, on the Bridegroom's behalf,
the insignia of the Golden Fleece and the Flying Lion.

The attendants who before had been invisible were now
visible to us, whereat I was exceedingly joyful. To those
others who had failed, and who were now seated at a lower

table, the attendants were still invisible.

When the meal was over, and a golden chalice sent by the Bridegroom had gone round, we new Knights of the Golden Fleece, seated on the steps of the Virgin's throne, were carried into the garden, to see those who had failed receive judgement. Here the Virgin led us by winding stairs into a gallery. But how the Emperor whom I had released behaved towards me here, I cannot relate for fear of slander.

And now that Virgin who had brought me my invitation, and whom I had hitherto never seen since, stepped forward and, giving one blast upon her trumpet, declared sentence on those guests who had been weighed and found wanting. Those who had weighed only a little too light were allowed to redeem themselves with gold and jewels, and to depart with dignity, receiving at the door the Draught of Forgetfulness. Some, who were lighter, were to be stripped and sent forth naked. Some, lighter yet, were to be scourged forth with rods and whips. Those who were proved imposters, and had never been invited, were to forfeit their lives to sword or halter.

Watching the execution of these sentences, I felt my eyes run over, till at last the garden, which had been so full, was emptied, and a silence fell upon it.

Into this silence delicately stepped a snow-white unicorn, a golden collar about his neck. He knelt in reverence before a lion who stood on a fountain with a naked sword held in his paw. The lion broke the sword, and the pieces sank into the fountain; then he reared till a snow-white dove came flying to him with an olive branch in her bill. This the lion devoured, and so was quieted; and the unicorn returned to his place with joy, while our Virgin led us back down the winding stairs.

When we had washed our heads and hands in the fountain, we each received from the Virgin a richly habited and learned page, able to discourse on all subjects, by whom we were conducted back into the Castle, and shown its paintings, treasures and antiquities. Many occupied themselves in copying the paintings; but I, on whom the page of greatest power had been bestowed, was led with my companion into parts of the Castle usually kept private, the keys of these having been committed to my page.

Here for several hours we stayed, seeing treasures none of the others were permitted to see, such as the Royal Sepulchre, with its glorious Phoenix, and a most noble Library. Though by now it had struck seven, and I began to feel the pangs of hunger, I was yet well content; I could be happy to fast all my life with such an entertainment.

When the King sent his page for the keys, we were shown a costly clockwork regulated according to the course of the planets; and next a huge terrestrial globe, on which we found our native lands marked with little rings of gold; others doing likewise, we discovered that our company was drawn from all parts of the Earth. This globe being hollow, we were able to sit within it and contemplate the stars glittering in an agreeable order in the interior of the Earth, and moving so gallantly that I had scarce any mind ever to go out again, as our page told our Virgin, and with which she twitted me, for it was already supper time, and I was almost the last at table.

At supper, as all grew merry with wine, the Virgin began to propound enigmas for which, try as we would, we could find no solution. She told us, for example: 'My sister and I have an eagle, whom we both cherish. One day we entered our chamber and found him with a laurel branch in his beak. I also had one in my hand; my sister had none in hers. The eagle went first to her, and gave her his branch, then came to me, motioning me to give him mine. Now whom did he love the better, my sister or myself?

The Virgin was become so familiar that I adventured and requested her name. Smiling at my curiousity, she replied in another riddle: 'My name contains 6 and 50, yet has only 8 letters. The third is a third part of the fifth which, added to the sixth, will produce a number whose sum will exceed the third itself by just the first, and which is half of the fourth. The fifth and seventh are equal. So are the last and first. The first and the second together equal the sixth, which contains four more than the third tripled. Now, my lord, how am I called?'

This answer was intricate enough; yet I left not off, but said: 'Noble and virtuous Lady, may I not obtain one only letter?'

'Yea,' said she, 'that may well be done.'

'What then,' I proceeded, 'may the seventh contain?'

'It contains,' said she, 'as many as there are lords here.'

With this I easily found her name, at which she was well pleased.

She now invited us to assist at the ceremony of Hanging Up the Weights. Six virgins entered, bearing lights and escorting a stately Duchess, less wordly than our Virgin, and looking up towards Heaven rather than towards Earth. We all took her for the Bride, but were much mistaken, although in honour, riches and state she much surpassed the Bride, and afterwards ruled the whole Wedding.

To me she said: 'You have received more than others; see that you also make a larger return.'

This to me was a very strange sermon.

Though the scales had been removed from the hall, the weights were still standing on their little table. The Duchess directed each of her virgins to take up one, and to our Virgin she gave her own, the largest and heaviest. The company then went in procession to seven chapels, in the first of which our Virgin hung up the Duchess's weight, while in each of the others one of the other virgins hung up hers; in all the chapels, led by the Duchess, we sang a hymn together and prayed that the Royal Wedding might be blessed.

Then each of us was conducted by his page to a richly furnished bedchamber, where the page lay on a pallet near him, in case he had need of anything in the night. This was the first night that I slept in quiet; and yet a scurvy dream would not suffer me to rest, for I was troubled with a door which I could not open, though at last I did so; and with these fantasies I passed the time till I awaked.

The Fourth Day

Next morning I over-slept my breakfast, they being unwilling to waken me because of my age; but I was soon ready with my habit, and found the rest assembled beside the fountain in the garden.

Today the lion on the fountain, in place of his broken sword, bore a tablet announcing that in its water Prince Mercury had a healing medicine for all ills, and concluding:

> Let him drink of me who is able,
> Let him who will, wash,
> Let him trouble me who dares,
> Drink, Brethren, and live.

When we all had washed in the fountain, and drunk of its water from a golden cup, we were given new garments of cloth-of-gold, gloriously set out with flowers, and a new insignia of the Golden Fleece, from which hung a disc of gold, with the sun and the moon on one side, and on the other this inscription: 'The light of the moon shall be as the light of the sun; and the light of the sun shall be seven times brighter than at present.'

Led by our Virgin with sixty virgins in attendance, and by musicians clad in red velvet, we mounted a winding staircase of 365 steps to the Royal Hall, where I saw the young King and Queen as they sat in their majesty amid unspeakable glory; for besides that the room glittered of pure gold and precious stones, the Queen's robes were so made that I was not able to behold them.

Our Virgin presented us to the King as wedding guests who had ventured hither at peril of body and life. It would have been fitting for one of us to have spoken somewhat on such an occasion but, seeing we were all troubled with a falling of the uvula, old Atlas, the Court Astrologer, stepped forward and welcomed us on the King's behalf.

The young King and Queen sat under a great arch at the western end of the hall; each wore a wreath of laurel, and over them hung a large and costly crown. On one side of them sat enthroned an ancient grey-bearded king with a fair young queen; on the other, a black king, middle-aged with a veiled and dainty old matron.

Cupid darted hither and thither; sometimes he seated himself between the two lovers; sometimes he made as if he would shoot one of us; he was so full of his waggery that he would not spare even the little birds, which flew about the chamber in multitudes. The virgins also had their pastimes with him; and when they could catch him, it was no easy matter for him to get from them again. Thus this little knave made all the sport and mirth.

Before the King and Queen stood a little altar, bearing six curious objects—a book bound with black velvet, overlaid with gold; a taper alight in an ivory candlestick, upon which Cupid now and then puffed in sport; a celestial globe, turning of itself; a chiming clock; a crystal fountain of red water; and a skull through whose eye-holes a small white snake wound in and out.

The audience over, the musicians played us down the winding stairs again to our own hall where, our mirth falling into our feet, virgins and lords struck up a civil dance together; after which we attended their Majesties through many stately walks to the House of the Sun, to see a merry comedy, the Duchess leading, carrying a small pearl crucifix, her six virgins carrying the sacred objects from the altar, and Atlas bringing up the rear.

The merry comedy opened with an ancient King sitting upon his throne; a little chest found floating on the sea was brought to him. In it he found the infant princess of a neighbouring kindom, who had been stolen by the Moors. He had her tenderly and royally brought up, and planned to marry her to his son when she came of age.

Again she fell into the hands of the Moors and was rescued by an ancient knight; she was restored to her lost kingdom and crowned queen. A third time, and now of her own free will, she fell into the hands of the Moor, who usurped her kingdom, stripped and scourged her, and cast her into prison.

The young king to whom she was betrothed made war upon the Moors on her behalf, and was victorious; he released the young queen, and restored her to her kingdom; they were married amid great rejoicings; and the play closed with a wedding hymn, calling down blessing on our King and Queen, and praying that a fairer future race might spring from them.

We now returned to the Royal Hall for the wedding feast. Though the tables were richly furnished, and all the royal persons were attired afresh in snow-white glittering garments, there was no music, the young King sighed often, the old King and Queen were grave, and all was performed with such state and solemn stillness, and all things had so strange a face, that foreboding of some imminent peril hung over us all.

Presently the young King took the black-bound book from the altar, and asked those of us who were resolved to keep faith with him to write our names in it. One after another, we all rose and did so. Then the crystal fountain of red water was brought, and with it a small crystal drinking-cup, from which the whole company drank the Draught of Silence, as in any House of the Mysteries.

At the tolling of a bell, the white garments were exchanged for black ones; floors, ceiling, walls, all were covered with black velvet. Our Virgin brought in six black taffeta scarves, with which she bound the eyes of the three Kings and the three Queens. The tables were removed, and six covered coffins placed in the centre of the hall, around a low black seat. Finally, in came a coal-black Moor, with a naked axe in his hand.

The old King was led to the low black seat, and there solemnly and reverently beheaded. His head was wrapped in a black cloth; his blood was caught in a golden cup; both were placed with his body in the first coffin. One after another, the other two Kings and the three Queens submitted with silent dignity to the same fate. Then the black executioner, preparing to withdraw, was himself beheaded, and his head placed with his axe in a little shrine.

To me this seemed indeed a bloody Wedding, and I and others wept; but our Virgin bade us be of good courage, telling us: 'The life of these Kings and Queens stands now in your hands; if you will but follow me, this death shall make many to live.'

She bade us all good-night, bidding our pages conduct us to our chambers. Mine alone looked out over the lake. About midnight, being unable to sleep, I became aware of a bright glow on the water and, rising from my bed, I saw seven ships sailing swiftly to the Castle, all full of lights. Over each ship hovered a flame. As soon as I saw them I knew: 'These are the spirits of the beheaded.'

As the ships drew gently to land, our Virgin went through the night to meet them, torch in hand; behind her came attendants, bearing the six covered coffins and the little shrine, which they placed one in each ship. I roused my page; together we saw all the lights but one of each ship go out, the flames pass again across the lake, and the Virigin return to the Castle, leaving hundreds of watchmen encamped along the shore, to keep guard through the night.

Then my page and I again retired to rest; and at last, being extremely weary, we both fell asleep.

The Fifth Day

Next morning, being awake long before the rest, I entreated my page to lead me a little about the Castle, and show me somewhat that was rare, whereupon he led me down an underground staircase to an iron door, on which was inscribed in copper letters: 'Here lies buried Lady Venus, the fair woman who hath undone many a great man.'

My page led me by the hand through this door and along a dark passage to another, normally kept locked, but unlocked today because the coffins had yesterday been brought out through it. Through it we reached the King's Treasury, a glorious vault which had no other light but from certain huge carbuncles, and where, my page told me, I would see things which no human eye outside the Royal Family had every seen till now.

In the middle of the vault was a rich tomb, like an altar, triangular in shape, supported by an ox, an eagle and a lion, and made entirely of gold and precious stones. On it, in a vessel of polished copper, stood an angel, bearing a tree in his arms. From this tree fruit fell continually into the vessel, turned there to water, and ran out into three smaller golden bowls.

Opening a copper door in the pavement, my page now led me down another exceeding dark staircase to an even deeper chamber. I was mightily terrified when he lit a torch from a small, ever-burning taper, and asked how he durst do this. He gave me for an answer: 'As long as the Royal Persons are still at rest, I have nothing to fear.'

In this chamber, by the light of the torch, I espied a rich bed hung about with curious curtains, one of which my page drew, and I saw the Lady Venus, stark naked (for he heaved up the coverlets too), lying there in such beauty that I was almost beside myself.

Behind the bed was a tablet, on which was inscribed: 'When the fruit of my tree shall be completely melted, then will I awake and be the mother of a King.'

When we ascended again to the King's Treasury, I there observed small tapers of pyrites, burning with flames so still and clear that I had mistaken them before for the precious stones. It was the heat from these that melted the fruit on the tree held by the angel, and cause more fruit continually to grow.

No sooner had we re-entered the Treasury than in flew the little Cupid, who promptly locked the copper door leading down to Venus's chamber, exclaiming: 'My old busy grandsire, you might lightly have served me a scurvy trick, had you been aware of this door. I must look better to it! Yet can I not let it pass unrevenged that you were so near stumbling upon my dear mother.'

And he heated the point of his dart in one of the taper-flames, and with it pricked my hand. I thanked God he had lighted on us no sooner, for at his unlooked-for appearance I felt more like the dead than the living.

I now joined my fellow-guests in our hall, where Cupid would needs have me show him my hand, where he still found a little drop of blood, at which he heartily laughed, and bade the rest have a care of me, as I would shortly end my days. We all wondered how he could be so merry and have no sense of yesterday's sad passages.

Our Virgin, dressed in black velvet, now conducted us to the garden, where we found six sepulchres under a roof supported by seven columns, above which floated a flag with a Phoenix painted on it. Here we assisted at the inter-ring of six coffins and a little shrine. The other guests throught they had been present at the royal funeral; only I knew differently.

Our Virgin now reminded us of our oaths of allegiance to the Bridegroom, and invited us to sail with her to the island Tower of Olympus, to assist in preparing the medicaments needed to restore the Royal Persons to life. We willingly followed her to the shore, where the seven ships still lay at anchor, five of them flying planetary signs, one a globe and one a pyramid. Here she assigned us to the various ships, which then set sail in this order: Foremost, A, the Pyramid, carrying the Moor's head, with twelve musicians making excellent music. Then B, C, D abreast, in which we were disposed, our Virgin and I being in C, which flew the Globe. Then the two stateliest ships, E and F, whose flags were the Sun and Moon, having no passengers. In the rear, G, were forty virgins.

From the lake we passed through a narrow strait into the sea, where sirens, nymphs and sea-goddesses swam to meet us. Our Virgin, having re-arranged her ships in a pentagon about the Sun and Moon, yielded to their entreaties, whereupon the sirens sang of love so delicately and sweetly that I no more wondered at Ulysses for stopping the ears of his companions; Cupid began to work with me, too, which tended little to my credit. This was the wound I received on my head in the dream.

Presently we sailed on, and after some hours came within sight of the Tower of Olympus. Its Warden, a very ancient man, came out in a gilded pinnace to receive us and conduct us to his island. This was a perfect square, with a great wall running all round it, two hundred and sixty paces thick. The Tower itself was as if seven round towers had been built one by another, yet the middlemost was somewhat higher, and within they all entered one into another.

At the gate of the Tower, we were led a little aside while the six coffins and the little shrine were brought in without any but myself noticing. Then we were taken into its underground laboratory, to wash herbs, crush precious stones and extract juices and essences, our Virgin being so busy with us, and so full of directions, that she knew not how to give us employment enough.

By nightfall these tasks were completed; a little broth and a little wine were distributed, and mattresses were laid on the laboratory floor. I could not sleep, but walked for a while in the garden where, coming to stone steps leading to the top of the wall, I mounted them, to contemplate the calm, moonlit sea and the starry sky.

Here I was much moved to observe a conjunction of the planets such as is seldom seen. Then, just before midnight, I saw the seven flames appear again far across the sea, and pass over it to the island, coming to rest above the spire of the central Tower.

Suddenly the winds rose, the sea grew rough, and cloud covered the moon. Hastily I stumbled back to the laboratory, where, lulled by a gently purling fountain, I quickly fell asleep.

The Sixth Day

Next morning the Warden of the Tower entered the underground laboratory, followed by youths carrying ladders, ropes and large wings. 'My dear sons,' he said, 'One of these three things must each one of you this day constantly bear about with him. To make choice you shall cast lots.'

My lot fell on a ladder, twelve foot long and pretty weighty; and I must be forced to carry it, whereas the others could handsomely coil their ropes about them, while as for the wings, the old man joined them so neatly on to the third sort as if they had grown upon them.

He then withdrew, taking with him the fruits of our yesterday's labours and locking the door behind him, so that we imagined we had been imprisoned in the Tower. But after a quarter of an hour, a round hole in the ceiling was uncovered from above, where we saw our Virgin, who bade us a cheerful goodmorrow, desiring us to come up. The winged sort were able to do so instantly. Those with ladders followed, each drawing up his ladder after him. But those with ropes had to wait until these had been suspended for them from iron hooks, and even then the ascent was not compassed without blisters.

The hole being covered again, we found outselves in a laboratory surrounded by six stately vestries, to which we were first directed, to pray for the life of the King and Queen. The twelve musicians who had sat in the ship of the Pryamid now brought in a fountain, and with it a great oval casket which, as I surmised, contained the bodies of the beheaded Kings and Queens. Then, while they played a most delicate voice of music, in came our Virgin, bearing the little shrine containing the Moor's head, and followed by veiled virgins with laurel boughs and torches.

All now stood round the fountain while our Virgin took from the little shrine the Moor's head, wrapped in taffeta, and placed it in a vessel, into which were then poured the essences and tinctures prepared yesterday. It was from the Moor's head that this solution conceived so great a heat, the virgins also placing their torches on spikes beneath the vessel, so that the water driving from the fountain seethed and simpered. Their laurel boughs they stuck into holes all round the fountain, so that the spray falling on them dropped into the vessel coloured a deeper yellow.

For two hours the fountain played, and the distillations dripped into the oval casket till the bodies it contained were quite dissolved. Then our Virgin had a golden robe brought in; into this ran a red liquid from the oval casket; then the globe was carried forth again.

We laborators now sat alone for a quarter of an hour or so, till I, perceiving a trampling overhead, had an eye to my ladder. The cover in the ceiling was lifted, and up we went by wings, ladders and ropes. It did not a little vex me that our Virgin could go up another way; yet I could judge we must leave somewhat for the old man (the Warden) to do.

And indeed, when we came up to this third conclave, we found the golden globe already suspended by a strong chain from the centre of the ceiling. The walls of this third laboratory were nothing but windows alternating with mirrors, so optically opposed that the sun was everywhere reflected, so that in all quarters of the room there was nothing but suns.

The heat from all these artificial refractions beat blindingly upon the golden globe, till our Virgin judged the desired temperature to have been reached. She gave orders now for the mirrors to be covered and, when the globe had cooled, for us to lift it down and cut it asunder. After much disputation, this was at last done with a diamond; and when the two halves fell apart, a great snow-white egg was disclosed, so beautiful that we stood around it as jocund as if we ourselves had laid it.

As soon as our Virgin was satisfied that the shell had sufficiently hardened, she carried the egg from the room, locking the door behind her. What she did abroad with the egg, I know not; we were again to pause for one quarter of an hour, till the third hole opened, and we, by means of our instruments, came up to the fourth floor.

Here we found a great square copper vessel, filled with silver sand, in which the egg was placed and warmed over the gentle fire till, being ready, it was taken out, but needed no cracking, for the Bird soon freed himself, looking very jocund.

Our Virgin warned us to tie him up before we fed him; this we did, setting him on the warm sand and bringing him the blood of the beheaded Kings and Queens to drink, whereupon he grew before our eyes, became covered with black feathers, and bit and scratched so devilishly that, could he have had his will upon any of us, he would soon have despatched us.

When we brought him other meat, he grew tamer and more tractable; he moulted his black feathers and replaced them with snow-white ones. At his third feeding, his feathers began to be so curiously coloured that I never saw the like for beauty, and he now behaved himself so friendly with us that, our Virgin consenting, we released him from captivity.

At dinner we began to make merry together, spending our time for the most part with our Bird; after which our Virgin and our Bird departed from us, and the fifth room was opened, which we reached after the former manner.

Here we found our Bird awaiting us, and a cool milky bath prepared for him, in which he pleasantly sported; as the lamps beneath it made it warmer, we had enough to do to keep him in the bath, and therefore clapped a cover on, suffering him to thrust out his head through a hole.

In this heated bath, the Bird lost all his feathers, which the water consumed, turning blue, and the Bird stepped out as smooth as a new-born babe. The bath we heated further, till all the water had evaporated, leaving only a blue stone; this we ground to powder, with which we painted the Bird blue all over, except for his head which remained white.

Again our Virgin departed with her Bird, and we ascended through the ceiling to the sixth conclave, where we found a little altar set up in the middle of the chamber, and on it the book, the lighted taper, the heavenly globe, the chiming clock, the crystal fountain, and the skull with its white serpent, every way like those in the King's hall.

The Bird stood on the altar, and drank from the blood-red fountain, then pecked at the white serpent till she bled. The heavenly globe turned till a certain conjunction was reached, then a second, then a third; after each conjunction the clock chimed.

Then the poor Bird himself submissively laid down his neck upon the book, and willingly suffered his head to be smitten off by one of us, thereto chosen by lot. Howbeit, he yielded not one drop of blood till he was opened on the breast, and then the blood spun out so fresh and clear as if it had been a fountain of rubies. His death went to the heart of us, yet we might well judge that a naked bird would stand us in little stead. We assisted the Virgin to burn the body (together with a little tablet hanging by) to ashes, with fire kindled at the little taper, and to lay them in a box of cypress wood.

Here I cannot conceal what a trick I, with three more, was served. 'My lords,' said the Virgin, 'we are here in the sixth room, and have only one more before us. I have found among you these four (pointing to me and three others) lazy sluggish laborators, and I purpose that they shall be excluded from the seventh and most glorious action.'

The virgin so well knew how to keep her countenance that the water of our grief soon ran over our baskets. The musicians were fetched and with cornets blew us out of doors with such derision that they themselves could scarcely sound for laughing. But as soon as we were come out of the door they bid us be of good cheer, and follow them up the winding stairs to the eighth floor under the roof, where we found the old man standing.

He received us friendly, and congratulated us that we were hereto chosen by the Virgin. When he had understood the fright we had conceived, his belly was ready to burst with laughing that we had taken such good fortune so heinously. 'Hence,' said he, 'my dear sons, learn that man never knoweth how well God intendeth him.'

Our Virgin, running in with her cypress box of the Bird's ashes, also joined in the laughter; and we four were set to work under the direction of the old Warden, moistening the ashes to a dough with prepared water, heating this paste, then casting it into two little moulds.

While this was cooling, we peeped through a crevice in the floor at our fellows, now busy on the storey below, where we saw them industriously blowing at furnaces and making gold, imagining they were herein wonderfully preferred before us.

When we opened our two little moulds, we found two bright and almost transparent little images, angelically fair babes, a male and a female, each being but four inches long. These we laid on two little satin cushions, and beheld them till we were almost besotted upon so exquisite an object.

Under the old man's direction, we let the blood from the Bird's breast fall drop by drop from a golden cup into their mouths, till they had reached their perfect full growth, with curled gold-yellow hair. The old man commanded us to lay them on a long table covered with white velvet, and to cover them with white taffeta which, because of their unspeakable beauty, it went hard with us to do.

Our Virgin now entered with two curious garments, which could have been crystal but that they were gentle and not transparent. These she laid upon a table; and while her musicians played, she and the old man performed many ceremonial gestures directed towards the roof. This was arched into seven hemispheres, and at the top of the middle and highest of these I spied a small aperture.

Now entered six virgins, each bearing a large trumpet, wreathed with a green, glittering, burning material. The old man took them one by one, placing them one after another

on the mouths of the two sleepers, with their wider ends
directed to the roof. Along each of the funnels thus made,
I saw a bright stream of flame shoot down from the aperture in the roof, and enter the sleeping image, which
immediately twinkled its eyes though scarcely stirring.

Next the two sleepers were neatly laid by each other in
a travelling bed, where they continued to sleep behind
drawn curtains. Meanwhile, we sat very still, attending
when our married couple would awake; and thus about half
an hour was spent. Then Cupid flew in, and tormented them
till they waked, which happened to them with very great
amazement, for they imagined that they had slept from the
hour in which they were beheaded; and when our Virgin
had clothed them in their new garments, all present kissed
their hands, and escorted them down the stairs and out to
the royal ship in which, with Cupid and a train of virgins,
they set sail for home.

At supper the Virgin brought us again to our former companions, where we were to carry ouselves as if we had truly
been in a lamentable condition. At this supper the old lord
was with us; I learned most by this old lord, and if men
would but take notice of his procedure, things would not
so often and untowardly miscarry.

After supper, the old lord led us into his closet of rareties,
where we saw such wonderful productions of Nature and
other things which man's wit, in imitation of Nature, had
invented, that we needed a year sufficiently to survey them.
Thus we spent a good part of the night by candle-light.

We then retired to handsome bed-chambers; and I, being
weary with continual labour, had good rest, continuing in
one dream from eleven of the clock till eight the next
morning.

The Seventh Day

Next morning, the morning of the seventh and last day, we
met in the nethermost vault of the Tower, and were given
habits entirely yellow, together with our golden fleeces, for
we were still dressed in our black funeral garb.

After breakfast, the old lord presented each one of us with a golden medal, bearing on one side the words, 'Art is the priestess of Nature,' and on the other, 'Nature is the daughter of Time.' So we went forth to the sea, where our ships lay, richly equipped. The ships were twelve in number, six of ours and six of the old lord's; but he betook himself to us in our ship, where we were all together. In the first the musicians seated themselves, of which the old lord had a great number. Our flags were the twelve celestial signs, and we sat in Libra. The sea was so calm that it was a singular pleasure to sail; but that which surpassed all was the old man's discourse, who so well knew how to pass away our time with wonderful histories that I could have been content to sail with him all my life long.

After two hours' sailing we passed from the sea into the narrow strait, and out of this into the lake, which we found covered with 500 ships which had sailed from the Castle to meet us, led by one sparkling with gold and precious stones, in which sat the young King and Queen, on whose behalf Old Atlas welcomed us.

The rest of our companions were in a huge amazement whence this King should have arisen, for they imagined no other than that they must again awaken him. We carried ourselves as if it seemd strange to us too. After Atlas's oration, out steps our old man, wishing the King and Queen all happiness and increase, after which he delivered a curious small casket, but what was in it I know not; it was delivered to the custody of Cupid , who hovered between them both.

So we sailed on a good time together, till we arrived at another shore, near the first gate at which I first entered. Horses awaited us there; and when we disembarked, the old lord and I rode with the young King, each of us bearing a snow-white ensign with a Red Cross; I, indeed, was made use of because of my age, for we both had long grey beards and hair. I had fastened my tokens round my hat, of which the young King soon took notice, and demanded if I were he who at the gate had redeemed these tokens. I answered yes in the most humble manner; but he laughed on me, saying there henceforth needed no ceremony, I was HIS Father.

When we reached the first Portal, the Guardian in his sky-blue habit awaited us, a supplication in his hand; this he delivered to me, begging me to use my good offices in laying it before the King. On the way to the second Portal, therefore, I asked the King about this Guardian, and he replied that he was a very famous astrologer but, having on a time committed a fault against Venus by beholding her in her bed of rest, this punishment was imposed upon him, that he should so long wait at the gate till someone should release him from thence.

'May he then be released?' I asked.

The King replied: 'Yes, if another commits the same transgression, he must take his place.'

This word went to my heart; conscience convinced me that I was the offender, yet I held my peace and delivered the supplication. As soon as the King had read it, he was mightily terrified; and as soon as we alighted, he called for Old Atlas to come to him in a little closet, and showed him the writing. Atlas made no long tarrying, but rode out to the Portal to take better cognizance of the matter.

It was now announced that after supper each of us could crave some boon of the King. Meanwhile the King and Queen began to play together a game not unlike chess, with the virtues and vices one against another, where it might be observed with what plots the vices lay in wait for the virtues, and how to re-encounter them. During the game, in comes Atlas again and makes his report in private; yet I blushed all over, for my conscience gave me no rest.

The King now handed me the supplication to read. In it the Guardian of the First Portal reported that his observations of the stars revealed that one of the King's guests had uncovered Venus; thus the time had come when he himself should be released from his office, and he begged to be permitted to be present at that evening's banquet in the hope of discovering his successor.

The King accordingly sent to invite him to join us; and as we sat at table he made his strict survey. Then certain curious chairs were placed in a circle in which we, together with the King and Queen, both their old men, and the ladies and virgins, were to sit. A handsome page then announced that the King, in recognition of our services, had elected each of us Knight of the Golden Stone, and required us to make these five vows:

I.   To ascribe our Order only to God and his handmaid, Nature.
II.   To abominate all whoredom, and not defile our Order with such vices.
III. To use our talents to assist all that have need of them.
IV.   Not to strive for wordly pride and high authority.
V.   Not to wish to live longer than God would have us.

At this last article we could not choose but laugh. But we were now with due ceremony installed Knights, and conducted in procession to a little chapel, where I hung up my golden fleece and my hat. And because everyone was to write his name there, I writ thus: 'The highest wisdom is to know nothing. Brother Christian Rosenkreutz, Knight of the Golden Stone, 1459.'

The King then retired to a little closet, to which each of us was to come in private, to request our boons. I decided, even at my own peril, to release the Guardian of the First Portal from his office; so, when I was called in, I made a full confession.

The King wondered mightily at this, and wished me to step aside a little; and as soon as I was called in again, Atlas declared to me that it was grievous to the King's Majesty that I, whom he loved above all others, was fallen into such mischance; yet, because it was not possible for him to transgress his ancient usages, the other must be released and I placed in his stead. Nor was my own release to be hoped for till the marriage feast of his future son. This sentence near cost me my life; yet I took courage, and related how this gate-keeper had been my benefactor, having bestowed a token on me by whose assistance I had stood upon the scale, and so had been made partaker of all the honour and joy already received. Hereupon the good man was pronounced free, and I imagined no other than that I must finish my life under the gate.

The ring of office was now placed upon my finger, and

the King embraced me, telling me this was the last time I would see him in this manner, from all of which I understood that in the morning I must sit in my gate. But when the time came to retire, and the rest of the Knights were conducted to their chambers, and I, most wretched man, had nobody to show me the way, who should approach me but the two august old lords—Atlas and the Warden of the Tower—who conducted me into a glorious lodging, in which stood three beds, and each of us lay in one of them. . .

* * * * * * *

At this point the narrative breaks off abruptly in the middle of a sentence, and this colophon is added: 'Here are wanting about two leaves in quarto; and he (the author hereof), whereas he imagined he must in the morning be the doorkeeper, returned home.'

Part Two

Commentary on the Story

The explanation of the story which follows draws in places on Rudolf Steiner's three articles published in *Das Reich* (October 1917 - April 1918) entitled 'The Chymical Wedding of Christian Rosenkreutz.'

The First Day (Saturday) [7]

The house of Christian Rosenkreutz is situated on a hill, a picture of higher consciousness. (We are reminded of Belmont, 'the beautiful mountain', the home of Portia in *The Merchant of Venice*.) It is a cottage, a picture of his simplicity and humility of soul, of which we shall hear much in the story.

While he is meditating, it seems to him that a great storm blows up. The act of meditation has lifted his consciousness to the etheric world, where all is in movement, in contrast to the still immobility of the physical world. This is the storm which sweeps the creative artist at the moment of creation when music, a poem, a picture, is conceived. It seems about to shatter his house to pieces—even his physical body is affected.

This heightened consciousness makes him aware of a spiritual being behind him. As he turns to look at her, light streams from his own being. Meeting this spiritual visitant, it is rayed back and gives him the impression of a blue mantle. All is not rayed back, however; and where it is absorbed by the being he has the impression of stars. Thus he pictures her in a blue, star-spangled garment.

The visitor bears in her hand letters in all languages, for her message is universal, and given to men all over the earth who are sufficiently mature to receive it. Christian Rosenkreutz does not follow the way of the mystic, but of the alchemist; while the mystic strives to come to spiritual truth by entering more deeply into his own being, the alchemist wishes to penetrate to the super-sensible which is hidden behind Nature. He knows that in order to do this he must develop a greater capacity for distinguishing between truth and illusion. This pilgrim, having heightened his sense for truth by uniting himself with the Christ Being, feels secure in his belief that this spiritual experience is a reality, because he sees on the letter the sign of the cross, and the words *in hoc signo vinces*. Because its contents are of very great spiritual importance to him, it feels heavier than gold.

In the letter he is told that he is is invited to a Royal Wedding 'by birth and by God's choice'; it lies in his destiny, but is also bestowed on him by grace. He is bidden to go to a place where three temples stand, whence he will see the direction he must take. He does not at the moment understand this, but he knows that a spiritual seeker has Imaginations from time to time which he has to allow to ripen within him until he is mature enough to understand them; if he tried to explain them intellectually he would spoil his apprehension of them. Seven years earlier, he had not understood an impression which came to him that he would one day receive an invitation to the wedding of a king. It is only now that he apprehends this experience.

He next makes a diligent search into the positions of the planets, and finds he may venture to hope for a spiritual experience at this time. It is important for him that it is Easter 1459, called in the story 'the year of balance', for he knows that human development must move harmoniously with earth evolution if it is to come about in the right way.[2]

However, he feels very unworthy and is still unsure whether he should go. He decides to ask his good angel to help him, and in this mood he falls asleep. Because his soul has already to a certain degree been transformed, his dreams are real experiences in the spiritual world. Many people have such experiences, but only those who are mature bring back a memory of them into waking life.

In the 'Tower of Blindness' he feels cramping and distress because his soul is trying to free itself from sense-experience. What binds the soul to the body are the forces of life and growth. But these do not give consciousness. This only arises because man takes into himself the forces of old age and death, which are portrayed in the story by the 'ice-grey man'. Only that soul can participate in the vision of the spiritual world who becomes aware of these forces which in everyday life are hidden behind age. This force has power to tear the soul away from the realm of sense-experience. Thus it is the ice-grey man who helps the prisoners to escape from the dungeon.

It is interesting that the prisoners who were heaving and struggling with one another in the depths are ready to help those who are less fortunate than themselves once they have attained the next higher stage of consciousness.

Each prisoner is brought by the ice-grey man before the 'Ancient Mother', the powers that lie behind Nature. As each leaves her she gives him a gold coin to spend by the way. On one side is a picture of the rising sun, and on the other D.L.S. (*deus lux solis*—God, the Light of the Sun). Henceforth all Nature will seem changed to them. The pilgrim will experience a new wealth of understanding and an awareness that a spiritual sun is hidden within Nature.

In this experience Christian Rosenkreutz has received wounds on the head and feet, and these he refers to later. The head-wound is spoken of in connexion with his experience with Venus. There is a mysterious connexion between the power of physical procreation and intelligence, the power of spirit creativeness. Man must transmute the former into the latter; failure to do so is like a 'wound in the head'. Later we shall see the meaning of this more fully.[8]

Of the wounds in the feet caused by the fetters, the Ancient Mother says to him, 'Keep these wounds for my sake'. It has been suggested that this mysterious saying has reference to the Washing of the Feet, an experience undergone early in Christian initiation. In the latter it is a training in humility, and we shall see how the humility of this pilgrim is of service to him in his future experiences. He must not forget what a struggle it was for him to get free of the body and thus receive a deeper understanding of Nature.

When Christian Rosenkreutz awakes he knows that he is allowed to make the journey and he arrays himself in his wedding garment. This is a white linen coat (we are reminded of the wedding garment of the guests in the parable). He wears a red stole crosswise, as a priest wears his. In the language of myth and fairy-tale this scissor-cross points to that human ego-consciousness which in man has a certain association with the crossing of the optic nerves which allows the eyes to focus and thus obtain clear sense-impressions beyond the scope of animals, with their parallel sight. (In fairy-tales the use of scissors shows this ego-consciousness in action, as when Red Riding Hood cuts open the wolf to release her grandmother.)

He also carries four red roses in his cap which he afterwards, at her request, gives to the Virgin who guides his initiation. These are symbols of his own inner development and show us that, for the true alchemist, alchemy consists above all in the transmutation of his own being. His giving these faculties to the Virgin indicates his wish to use them in the service of the spiritual word.[9]

He then takes bread, water and salt and sets out joyously on his way. Salt is a picture of his thinking, water of his feeling, and bread of his will. We shall see how he has to surrender these personal qualities as he penetrates more and more deeply into the spiritual world.

The Second Day (Sunday)

It is Easter Morning when Christian Rosenkreutz sets out on his initiation journey. This is the day on which Christ created His Resurrection Body, and our traveller (to take the story on a higher level of meaning) is setting out to undergo an experience which will enable him to create a copy of this body for himself.[10]

He remembers the golden token of his dream, whereby he was to see Nature henceforth in a new way; and he goes on his way rejoicing, because all Nature seems reborn. At length he reaches an open space where there are three mighty cedar trees. In the margin of the original story 'Three Templa' are spoken of at this point. We know that the Templum was a sacred spot dedicated to a god—in this case to Mercury, for his sign is on a tablet nearby. A Templum was also a place for taking auspices—this happens here in

the incident of the dove and the raven. So now we understand the 'three temples' to which the letter directed him
to go in order to find his further road. Mercury was also
the God of Travellers, and Christian Rosenkreutz is setting
out on a journey.

The traveller is confronted by four roads and is greatly
troubled to know which to take, especially as the tablet tells
him that, whichever he chooses, there is no turning back.
The first is rocky and dangerous, for the arid rocks of dry
materialism give rise to deceit. A spiritual seeker has to be
very mature to tread this road in safety.

The second is a long but safe road, the way of earthly
life, the way of faithful and patient meditation that leads
slowly but surely to the goal, provided that the traveller
turns neither to the right nor to the left. The one temptation
leads to neglect of earthly tasks in unrealistic dreaming—
this is called, in Spiritual Science, the way of Lucifer, the
deviation to the left. The deviation to the right leads astray
into so deep an immersion into material things that anything
spiritual seems to have no reality—this is the way of
Ahriman.

The third path is the Royal Road, by which men who have
attained maturity in a previous incarnation can quickly and
easily find their way to the Spirit. The fourth, encompassed
by fire and cloud, could only be traversed by those who
were not in the flesh; it is fit only for incorruptible
bodies.[11]

Christian Rosenkreutz sits down, bewildered and doubtful
as to which road he should take, and begins to eat his bread.
At once the snow-white dove flutters down, the messenger
of peace and love, and he shares his bread with her. We
may say his will is put at the disposal of this messenger of
the spirit. But the raven who molests her is also a messenger
from the spiritual world—we remember the ravens of Elijah
and that the Raven was the first degree in certain initiations.

Pursuing the two birds in his endeavour to help the dove,
the traveller finds himself already on the second road. Such
a choice cannot be taken by the conscious mind, and we
know that the events of seeming mischance may be
messengers leading us to take a step in the right direction.

Christian Rosenkreutz feels pity and love for the bird, and these feelings are often a surer guide than intellectual judgement. He turns round and considers going back; but so strong a wind blows up against him that he sees it would be impossible. Once embarked on an occult path, the spiritual seeker may not turn back. He finds that he has left his bread—his personal will—behind him.

So he keeps faithfully along this road all day long, travelling south, following the direction of the dove's flight, and using his magnet (compass) so that he may err neither to right nor left. There is a very beautiful diagram in the book of the *Secret Symbols of the Rosicrucians* which shows us the significance of the magnet in the story. It portrays a hand holding a Magnet Stone with the inscription: 'I attract all those seeking God and the Truth. I am the Magnet Stone of Divine Love, attracting the iron-hard men on the road to the truth.'

When Christian Rosenkreutz reaches the Castle he has to pass the three gates which lead into Imagination, Inspiration and Intuition. These names are given in Spiritual Science to three degrees of heightened awareness towards which every human being can train himself. It becomes possible to pass from a physical seeing to a seeing which is based on the activity of an inner light—a sense-free perception which enables one to become aware of the etheric body and also of happenings in the etheric world. This is the capacity of imaginative perception, or Imagination. This term for a quite exact and reliable *seeing* should not be confused with the term *imagination*, loosely used for any fantasy.

A further faculty of the mind, a faculty which allows us to become aware of our own astral body and of events in the astral world, is called Inspiration. This is a further development of the faculty of hearing, in the same way that Imagination is an extension of the sense of sight. It would take too long to go into the question here of why awareness of the astral is connected with sound. The reader may like to make reference here to *Man or Matter* by Dr Ernst Lehrs.

There is a third faculty which enables a man to be fully conscious of his own Ego, and also to enter into the being of others and to become cognizant of spiritual beings. To describe this gift Rudolf Steiner chose the word Intuition. Again, this must not be confused with the dim feeling often called by that name.

At the first gate he meets the Guardian, an elderly man whose blue mantle is a picture of devoted service. On the seventh day we see the full significance of this meeting, and of his warm greeting to the Rosicrucian Brother. The latter has to give up his water—his personal feeling—in order to obtain the token which will allow him to pass into the imaginative world; for in the realm of Imagination the man who works out of his personal feeling and fantasy will be led astray.

By this time it is dusk, and he is relieved to meet a beautiful Virgin who carries a flaming torch which lights the way for him. A seeker's first steps into the spiritual world are in part lit by a spiritual being, who comes to aid him, responsive to his need. At the gate he is confronted by a terrible lion, a picture of his own being as it appears in the etheric world in which he now finds himself. It is also a revelation to him of how he appeared before he came down into the sense-world. In the physical world, the life of instincts, impulses and emotions is held in chains to the man's ideas and thoughts. In the etheric world the true nature of his being is portrayed to him in this raging lion. Speaking in purely psychological terms, we might say that he has to face his subconscious being, which is to be transmuted by his further experiences.

At this point Christian Rosenkreutz has to surrender his salt (his power of personal thinking), for he is entering the realm of Inspiration. Again he must depend on the help of the Virgin, for as yet his powers are not strong enough to create the light by which he can find his way. As he reaches the last portal, the gate is suddenly clapped to, so that he has to leave behind his cloak, which is caught in the door. When we enter the spiritual world we must lay aside the cloak of our ordinary consciousness, which serves us well enough in everyday life. The keeper of the third gate gives the traveller a new pair of shoes—he has now to tread the ground beneath his feet in quite a different way. He gives his old shoes to a beggar for, as new spiritual gifts are given to us, we must continually pass on to others what we have received.

Now he finds he is to be tonsured. Hair is connected with natural, atavistic clairvoyance, as we recall in the story of Jacob and Esau, 'the hairy man'; it was the hairless Jacob who bore the forces of the future within him. The old clairvoyance, dependent on the organism, has to be surrendered in order that a new spirituality may develop. But the shaving of the head also uncovers the fontanel, by which pure spirit can later, when he has consciously and over a long period prepared himself, pour into a man's being.

The guests are now summoned to a banquet, and Christian Rosenkreutz is surprised to find such a large assembly of all sorts and conditions of men—including some acquaintances of whom he has never thought very highly. When he inquires how they have come, they mostly tell him they have travelled by the rocky road, the road of barren intellectualism, but also of corrupt occultism. These people are now scrambling for all the best places, and there is scant room at the lowest table for him and the other more modest members of the party who do not push forward.

At this point he makes friends with a 'fine quiet man', and hereafter always refers to him as 'my companion', 'my friend', 'my brother'.[12]

The beings of the spiritual world are as yet invisible to him and to most of the guests; and one who pretends to be able to see those who are serving them receives speedy punishment. The unworthy guests boast that they can see the Platonic Ideas, hear the movement of the planets, and so on. They have considerable intellectual knowledge of the occult but have not transformed their soul powers, and so have to pretend to experiences which are not real for them. To see these would-be guests sitting at the top table and boasting of their achievements makes Christian Rosenkreutz bitter and ironic. He says, 'This was part of the lameness I experienced in my dream.' We remember that the wounds on his feet were caused through the fetters by which the soul was held to sense-experience, though it struggled to get free. It would seem that he is still vulnerable through sense-experience, for when he is scorned by other guests whom he knows to be of less value than himself he is hurt by it. He recognizes sadly that his humility is not complete.

But the mood of our traveller changes when a new experience recalls to him the holiness and wonder of the Castle. There is beautiful music, and no-one speaks for the space of half an hour. We are reminded of the 'silence in heaven for the space of half an hour' before the opening of the seventh seal in the Apocalypse. There must always be a 'creative pause' to prepare the mind for something new which is about to take place.

The entrance of the Virgin is most impressive, and we realize for the first time the importance of her role as Initiator of the wedding guests. After welcoming them, she warns them of the test that awaits them next day, then allows them to make their own judgement of their own worth by either accepting a bed-chamber for the night or, if they feel unworthy, spending the night in the hall. Only Christian Rosenkreutz and eight others remain there, among them his new friend. It is just this sense of humility which enables him, during the following days, to develop spiritual power.

The binding of the pages is a picture of his feeling of spiritual impotence, which leads him to feel fettered. It is important to notice the functions of the virgins and the pages. The female beings portray spiritual beings—help given from the spiritual world—while the young males, the pages, are a picture of the will impulses arising in the soul. Thus the feeling of being bound arises from within, and is not due to any action by those in the Castle.

During the night he has a dream. Those who are hanging high have a shameful fall, and those who are hanging only a little way above the earth fall gently. He has a feeling that the meaning is that those who have made such vain boasts will be put to shame, and those who have been more modest, even if they do not pass the test, will at least not be so deeply disgraced. Awaking, he tells his friend of the dream, and is assured that it was sent to him for comfort. They feel that they and their seven companions have chosen the better part. It is right that they have felt the fetters of soul impotence in face of the spiritual world, for this feeling of powerlessness will later be transformed into power.

The Third Day (Monday)

The day opens with the testing of the guests. They are to be weighed on scales of gold, for the test concerns not head knowledge, but knowledge that has become heart wisdom, and gold concerns the heart.

The weights are the Seven Liberal Arts: *Grammatica, Rhetorica, Dialectica, Arithmetica, Geometrica, Musica and Astronomica,* through the study of which, up to the fifteenth century, students were trained. They were meant as an education towards the Spirit. The Quadrivium, the four last named, was already a way of initiation in ancient Egyptian Mystery Schools. Later the Trivium was added, for instance in the schools of Plato. Grammar was then thought of as the revelation of man as spirit through the word; Rhetoric was the revelation of man through the beauty of the word; and Dialectic, the revelation of the soul through forms of thought.

In earlier times seven living Goddesses stood before the soul; later they were presented to the student as pictures, and finally dried out into abstractions. Even up to the seventh century the pupils could learn to become aware of a mighty living Being, the Goddess Natura (described as the Ancient Mother in our story), who appeared before them in her full radiance and taught them the secrets of Nature. In the Christian Mystery Schools, she was spoken of as the Handmaid of Christ. The pupils did not learn of abstract laws of Nature but of the creative power of the Goddess Natura. She it was who led them to a knowledge of minerals, plants, animals and the elements as filled with divine power and substance. Only then were the pupils taught Astronomica—how through a knowledge of the wandering stars they could learn the secrets of the soul; and through that of the fixed stars, the secrets of the ego.[13]

It is remarked that the weights are heavy out of all

proportion to their bulk—the knowledge conveyed opens up in the true student profound vistas of wisdom. One can easily understand Grammatica, the revelation of the Word; Musica, the harmony of the spheres; and Astronomica, the star-wisdom which was a revelation of man's relation to the heavens, being spoken of as the weightiest of all.

In the case of Christian Rosenkreutz and the eight others who pass the tests, the knowledge has so ripened in them as to give them the weight of soul necessary for the experiencing of initiation into the spiritual world. The rejected guests, especially the intruders, have merely acquired intellectual knowledge—they have come 'the rocky way'. Some of them are even charlatans who have misled other guests by claiming bogus wisdom. Andreæ has much to say of the impostors in his own day who reaped fortunes from the credulous by such false occult claims.

The first Emperor can only sustain the first six weights—perhaps one could say he has not fathomed the implications of star-wisdom. There is only one Emperor who stands the test, and this one is described as a short man with a curly brown beard. As the test goes on we see how very high is the standard required by the spiritual world of the would-be candidate for initiation. At length only those are left who have spent the night fettered in the great hall; and of these only the Rosicrucian Brother and his friend are found not wanting. The former can support not only all the weights, but also these together with three men in armour.

On seeing this, one of the pages cries out loudly, 'This is he!'—that is the one for whom the wedding is consummated, the other guests in a sense being witnesses of the ceremony. Since the pages are a picture of the will-impulses arising in the soul, the cry of the pages is to be thought of as a sudden leaping up of self-consciousness, a piece of self-knowledge.

Christian Rosenkreutz is told that, because he has more than enough weight to pass the test, he may help one of those who have failed. He chooses the first Emperor, who had been so shattered by his failure. One is allowed to pass on spiritual wisdom to help another in need, just as one man helps another in the physical world. But whereas a material gift leaves the donor poorer, a spiritual gift blesses him that gives and him that takes. It is sad to read a little later that the Emperor repays his kindness by very scurvy treatment.[14]

It is at this point that the Virgin asks for Christian Rosenkreutz's four red roses, and is given them—he dedicates to the service of the spirit all that he has so far gained in occult development.

We notice that during this ceremony the Virgin and her attendants are clothed in crimson, and that as each successful guest takes his seat on her throne, he too is given a crimson mantle. Crimson is the colour of selfless love and we realize that, however stern the tests, they are made through love alone. The mantle of which the successful guests are found worthy reveals that no other soul-qualities are of avail without it. A mood of love suffuses the banquet, for the table is also decked in this same crimson. After these experiences the chosen few are able to see the servitors who were invisible to them the previous night—they have already attained a measure of clairvoyance.

The king sends them the insignia of the Golden Fleece and the Flying Lion. The Golden Fleece signifies that they have transformed their feeling-life, and the vehicle of the feelings shines like pure gold, as in the days when man had not yet fallen. The Flying Lion would seem to indicate the power of the feelings to soar upwards to the spirit.

After the conclusion of the meal, they all repair to the courtyard where justice will be meted out to the unsuccessful guests and impostors. It is at this point that Christian Rosenkreutz remarks on the ill-treatment given to him by the rejected Emperor whom he had helped.

Those who are genuine but not yet mature are sent away with dignity and given a Draught of Forgetfulness. On returning to ordinary life they will not remember what has happened to them; something of the kind happens to most of us every morning when we awaken from sleep. The impostors are so severely punished that the Rosicrucian Brother weeps at the sight. We realize that human judgements are very different from those of the world of the spirit, and that perfect love can be more stern than human weakness can understand.

The Rosicrucian Brother now finds dawning within him the power to see his intelligence in a way that is new to him. This appears before him as an Imagination of a unicorn. This wonderful creature is a picture of pure clairvoyance (for this reason it can only be caught by a pure maiden). It is a white horse (pure intelligence), with a horn which grows from a jewel in its brow (the two-petalled lotus-flower).[9] There is no earthly substance it cannot pierce, and nothing that this creature cannot see, for his power is supersensible. The unicorn kneels before the lion, who breaks a sword, the pieces of which sink into the fountain. The purified thinking bows before the feelings and calms them, but the two are not yet one, as they will be later.

Each guest now purifies himself further by washing head and hands in the fountain, and is then given a page to conduct him round the Castle. We have seen that the page represents a spiritual activity of the one he is serving, and so we recognize that each guest is now left to his own initiative as he penetrates further into the spiritual world. Some occupy themselves in copying the paintings—they think that what is required of them is faithfully to reproduce the beauty that has already been created. Christian Rosenkreutz has a more powerful page who has the key to those parts of the castle not usually shown.[15]

He and his companion visit the grave of the kings with its glorious Phoenix—a picture of the mysteries of death and transformation through a sacrificial act that leads to re-birth. Andreæ wants to describe how *The Chymical Wedding* stands at a special turning-point of time. The old way of initiation has died, and the new rises from the grave of the old. For all new developments must be founded on what has been right and good in the past.

The Rosicrucian Brother and his companion learn that to become the leaders of the modern age they must not go the old way of initiation with the help of the hierophant, but through voluntary self-sacrifice come to a re-birth such as will be consummated in the 'wedding' they are soon to witness. Thus they approach the developments of the following days with open and expectant hearts.

Nevertheless, the spiritual seeker has to enrich his soul

through a knowledge of the past evolution of man—hence their visit to the Library, the Akashic Record.

The king sends his page to get the keys back from their page—the rulers of the Castle would prefer spiritual life to continue along the old lines. Dr Steiner remarks here that even today the spiritual investigator finds that his strongest opponents are those who want to continue an old way of approach to the spiritual world.

Christian Rosenkreutz and his companion now visit the great globe and are interested to see that the rings which mark the home of each wedding guest are scattered all over the globe. This indicates that the new wisdom is universal, and not confined to either east or west. As they sit at the centre of the globe they see the power of the planets working within the earth—they learn the secrets of the seven metals which have been called the 'deeds of the planets within the earth.'[16]

Christian Rosenkreutz is so entranced that he can hardly tear himself away, and is laughed at for his tardy arrival at supper.

While they are eating and drinking, the Virgin propounds a riddle and asks the guests to find the answer. Then some of the guests do the same. In each case, the intellect can find no solution. Andreæ wants to show that in the spiritual world the human power of judgement must be suspended. Reality is richer than can be surmised by judgement based on sense experience.

Christian Rosenkreutz is now emboldened to ask the Virgin her name. From her indications he works it out as follows:

First letter	1	=	A
Second	12	=	L
Third	3	=	C
Fourth	8	=	H
Fifth	9	=	I
Sixth	13	=	M
Seventh	9	=	I
Eighth	1	=	A

Her name is Alchimia. We are invited to consider her being more closely. She is the imaginative representation of spiritual knowledge. Andreæ wants to show how true alchemy is concerned with the transformation of spiritual substance into physical and how a true understanding of physical substance leads to the supersensible. We now understand that it was Alchimia who led Christian Rosenkreutz with a torch as he drew near to the Castle, when the approach to the spiritual world seemed dark. True alchemy throws light on the pathway to the spirit.

And now there enters a very stately figure who reveals herself as Theologia. This Duchess is more other-worldly than Alchimia. One must not think of her in terms of the rather dry picture called up by the world 'theology' today, but rather see her as the earthly reflection of Sophia, Divine Wisdom. Her way is the way of faith, Alchimia's the way of knowledge. She looks towards heaven; Alchimia seeks to penetrate the secrets of earth.

The guests take her for the Bride, but in honour and riches Theologia much surpasses her. The Bride is the Higher Ego of Christian Rosenkreutz, the Duchess a reflection of the Cosmic Wisdom which reunites Man to God. For this reason her weight is the heaviest of all. It is given to Alchimia, for this heavenly wisdom borne by earthly wisdom gives perfect enlightenment. She reminds our Rosicrucian Brother that he has received most, so most will be expected of him. He finds this very strange—his humility always forbids his understanding how great his spiritual wisdom really is.

Each of the weights, which we have come to know as the Liberal Arts, is hung in a chapel—knowledge is dedicated to the service of God. The guests then pray for a blessing on the Royal Wedding.

Christian Rosenkreutz's dream in the night is of a door which needs great effort before he can open it. This is to remind him that his experiences so far are not of intrinsic value, but that they have helped to generate a force which will need to be strengthened by still greater effort on his part if he is to go further in his quest.

The Fourth Day (Tuesday)

This is the middle day of the seven, the heart of the story. It opens with a visit to the Fountain, which we now recognize as the Fountain of Healing and Inspiration, presided over by Mercury. The lion is redeemed; he is now the servant of Mercury; hence, after bathing in these healing waters, the guests are given new insignia of the Golden Fleece—they have achieved a greater purification of the feeling-life. This garment is covered with flowers—a reminder that the future body of man will be more flower-like in its texture, and will shine more brightly; at the same time, the moon and the sun will shine more brightly too.

Christian Rosenkreutz has now to face his own soul powers—he has to mount three hundred and sixty-five steps, perhaps a picture of a cycle of faithful, daily meditation; self-knowledge is not easily or quickly to be achieved. He meets three kings and their consorts—thinking, feeling and willing together form the foundation for conceptual life. Dr Steiner also speaks of them as the powers of memory and ideation on either side of the ego. The very old king would then represent the power of memory—a human faculty acquired in the dim past—wedded to the etheric life-forces which, as we know, grow younger as the physical organism grows older.

The black king may be thought of as the power of intellectual thinking, in which the light of wisdom has been darkened. The female counterpart of this is the intuition of the woman's mind, a delicate and veiled apprehension of ideas which a man's brain seizes in a more concrete way. This power of intuition was active in very ancient times; hence the queen is described as a 'dainty old matron'. The young king and queen represent, perhaps, the first dawn of imaginative thinking, to which only the ego can give birth.

The guests are welcomed by Atlas, the being who bears the burden of the earth on his shoulders. He receives them gladly because the transformation of even one individuality awakens in him the hope that one day his burden will be lightened, for the initiate works upon himself not for his own sake, but to help mankind and the earth. 'Man is the Messiah of Nature,' said Novalis, and the events of the sixth and seventh days reveal the depth of meaning in his words.

The symbols on the altar are very ancient Mystery tokens, showing man's connexion with the universe. The book points to the thought-content of man, the influx of world-creative thought into the soul. Through the little light it is indicated that world-thoughts are active in the world-ether and give illumination to men. Cupid blows upon the light—light and love are the two polar opposites which are active in all growth and becoming. The sphere indicates how man is interwoven with spatial existence, as the clock speaks of his connexion with cosmic time. The fountain from which blood-red liquid flows, and the death's head with the serpent, show how birth and death appear to the spiritual seeker as founded in the cosmos. The power of planets and zodiac interweave to bring about the life and destiny of man.

The comedy which is played represents the story of the soul of man during a lifetime, but also, on a second level, the development of the soul during earth evolution. Taking it in its simplest meaning, we see how birth is, as often, represented as an infant borne to solid ground in the waters of the etheric (we are reminded of the story of Moses in the bulrushes). As the king takes the child out of the water, he comments that she has previously been stolen by the Moor. In this connexion Rudolf Steiner speaks, in *Planetary Spheres*, of the way in which the power of evil (called Ahriman in occult literature) often fastens on the brain of a soul on its way into incarnation.

The princess is royally brought up by ancient wisdom, but at puberty she falls again into the hands of the Moor. She is rescued by an ancient knight—still working out of the good forces of the past—and is restored to her kingdom. When she comes of age she falls once more into the hands of the dark power—this time of her own free will—and is brutally ill-treated. The young prince, her higher self, has to conquer, not only the Moor, but also her own weakness and folly, before she is fit and able to become his bride. When at last higher and lower self are united, the multitude pray that from them a fairer race may spring. (We have echoes of part of this story in Shakespeare's *The Winter's Tale* and *The Tempest*.)

But now the dread moment approaches when the consciousness of the spiritual seeker must go through death in order to attain new life. At every step forward in occult development, it is necessary to overcome fear; and at this point a nameless fear overcomes Christian Rosenkreutz and the guests. The young king, the consciousness of the spiritual seeker, exacts an oath of faithfulness from his guests. We have spoken of the way in which this story must be read on many levels; and at this point the guests, in one sense perhaps representing concretely the stage attained by the greatest of earth-initiates, are to be thought of in another sense, as the nine members of man's being, each of which has been brought to a special perfection by one of the 'guests'. The whole being of man must take part in his regeneration, else his lower nature will betray him; hence the oath of fealty given to the young king. As Alchimia says, 'the life of the king, and many more, stand now in your hands.' Christian Rosenkreutz is to lead humanity into a new age.

The beheading signifies, on one level, the sacrifice of the forces of ideation and memory in order that a new, living thinking may be created. In another sense, it is the physical body that is to be regenerated in order to become the 'resurrection body' which is the gift of Christ to the future. After the six have been beheaded by the Moor (who is the same figure of evil as we have seen in the play), he himself suffers the same fate. He is a picture of the Judas individuality, who again and again has to act as 'the betrayer', the agent of a tragic fate, which nevertheless is a necessity in the working-out of karma. Yet it *is* an act of betrayal, and brings punishment in its train. The head of this being is gathered up and is a necessary ingredient in the alchemy by which the king and queen are given new life. A mysterious admixture of darkness belongs to the creation of new light.

The fate of the kings reminds us of the beheading of John the Baptist, who thus sacrifices the first half of the evolution of the earth, during which man developed the power of intellectual thinking. From the grave of this thinking is to arise the power of living thinking. Through this sacrifice and the uniting of his being with the power of the Christ Being, John the Baptist was able to play an important part in the unfolding of the new age.

At this point Rudolf Steiner speaks at length of how the two soul-forces, memory and ideation, are dependent on the same kind of physical condition as growth. But the forces of growth bear within them the forces of decline and death; therefore they can only give rise to dead thinking. Thus the spiritual seeker must realize in the foundation of his soul-processes the metamorphosis of the growth-processes in his body. Usually these life forces are only changed into cognitional forces by taking death into themselves. This is Nature's alchemy. The spiritual seeker has to carry this alchemy further.

To do this he must realize that, just as in the development from flower to seed certain forces are held back in order to produce something new, so the higher forces of knowledge have been held back as a seed, at the point where Nature has developed knowledge forces for what is dead. The next step, to awaken *living* forces of cognition, must be carried out by the would-be initiate himself. Such an achievement is 'a further shoot of renewed life in the being of the world.'[17]

Christian Rosenkreutz sleeps in a room which looks out over a lake—the etheric world. He has already achieved something of the consciousness which will be the possession of the man of the future. During the night he sees the seven flames of the seven beings who have lost their lives hover above the ships which are to bear the bodies to the place of resurrection. He is the only one who sees this for, after all, it is *his* forces that are undergoing the change. He sees that the Castle in which he is staying is well guarded by many watchmen, just as the temple of the body is guarded at night by spiritual beings. So, at long last, he falls asleep.

The Fifth Day (Wednesday)

Christian Rosenkreutz has now to penetrate into the realm of Venus, the source of life. We must recall what was said concerning the task of the initiate who seeks to bring life into his thinking. He must penetrate into the processes of Nature to the point at which she brings forth life. This is a dangerous realm, the realm of the Lady Venus, where Nature works with the force of love to produce new life. This realm is underground, because as yet Venus still works in the sphere of the unconscious will-forces. It is all too easy for the seeker to be overcome by the instincts unless his heart is filled with the purity of Christ. While Christian Rosenkreutz passes safely through this test, he nevertheless fears he has committed a grave fault in seeing the Lady Venus, whereas for these forces to be raised to consciousness was legitimate in the *new* initiation, though not in earlier times.

He first sees the tree of Venus, on an altar-like stone supported by the three beasts who traditionally represent thinking, feeling and willing—the eagle, the lion and the bull. The fourth being, man, the synthesis of the three, is not represented—but above is the angel, the higher nature of man, holding the fallen tree of life. The decaying fruit continually falls, melted by the flame of pyrites, which may be said to represent the sacrifice of Christ. It must become completely liquid—etheric; this liquid falls into golden vessels. The tablet by the side of Venus is inscribed: 'When the fruit of my tree shall be completely melted, then will I awake and become the mother of a king.' When the way of procreation has been completely transformed and purified, love will bring forth man worthy of the name of king.

The guests are now to view death from the earthly side—after death the interring of the remains is a sad task. Only Christian Rosenkreutz, through the experiences of the night, knows the truth, that the coffins are but empty shells, and that the beings who died the previous day are already on their journey to the place of re-birth. The guests are given an indication of what is to come by the flag bearing the picture of the Phoenix, always a symbol of resurrection.

The guests are now reminded of their oath of allegiance to the young king and invited to sail with Alchimia to the Isle of Olympus. Olympus, the Heaven of the Greek gods, and in particular of Jupiter, is the sun-filled ether-sphere. It will be noted that the ships set forth in the configuration of the cross and triangle. The foremost is the bearer of the Moor's head—the sign of the Pyramid seems to indicate that a solid grounding on the earth is necessary even for the most spiritual transformation of man's being. The next three ships form the cross-beam, as it were, of the cross; these are Mars—Earth—Mercury (see Note 2, paragraph 3). Christian Rosenkreutz is naturally on the ship bearing the sign of the Globe (Earth) for he is concerned wholly with earth-development. The virgins in the ship behind bear laurel branches. Their ship carries the sign of Venus; the laurel, an emblem of sun-filled thinking, prefigures the future—the redeemed Venus-power. This ship with Sun and Moon make the triangle. As the cross is the sign of earth-life, so is the triangle an emblem of heaven. Jupiter is not represented, for it is to the Island of Jupiter, the Isle of Olympus, that they are bound. Jupiter is the laboratory of the gods, the home of Plato's Ideas, which are there formed before coming into physical manifesation.

Before the Virgin gives permission for the sirens to sing to the voyagers, she changes the formation of her little fleet, which now makes a pentagon as if protecting the ships bearing the bodies of the kings, which fly the signs of the Sun and Moon. The pentagon encloses the pentagram, which in an occult sense is the image of the perfect man of the future—the Mercury man to be developed in the second half of earth-evolution.

The sirens—primal love—who belong to the realm of the Father, are then allowed to sing their sweet but seductive song. It moves even the Rosicrucian Brother in such a way that he remarks, 'This was the wound in my head.' We are again reminded of the mysterious connexion between ideation and the reproductive powers.[8]

As they draw near to the Tower of Olympus the Ancient Warden comes out to greet them. We have seen that the

island is situated in the sea of the etheric. It is square in
form, the perfection of the earth-form; we are reminded
of the New Jerusalem, which also was 'four-square'. On the
island is a Tower, the hidden laboratory of the Powers of
Creation. In this Tower the work of regeneration will take
place. It has a ground-plan of seven interlacing circles, the
plan of many ancient Mystery temples, and stands seven
storeys high.[18] This is a picture of the sevenfold being of
man, and also, on another level, of the seven epochs of
earth-development, in the course of each of which one
vehicle of the soul of man was to be developed. Seven has
always to do with earthly time, just as twelve is the number
of space.

The guests are now set to work in an underground
laboratory at their first task, which is the preparation for
use of herbs and crystals. This is Nature's alchemy, which
has to be faithfully carried out before the spiritual seeker
can bring about something new.

When night falls, Christian Rosenkreutz goes out into the
garden and looks up at the stars. He is delighted to see a
conjunction of the planets which gives him confidence that
their enterprise is rightly timed. He then sees the seven
flames of the dead persons cross the ocean and come to rest
over the top of the Tower, where their souls will await the
new bodies which are to be prepared for them.

The Sixth Day (Thursday)

This is Thursday—*jeudi*, the day of Jupiter, the day of new
creations. The experiences of this day are the core of the
whole initiation.

Concerning the pictures in which these experiences are
conveyed to us by Andreæ, Rudolf Steiner says that they
are in a sense unimportant, since another occultist could
have conveyed the same process in different pictures. What
is important is what happens in the soul of the reader as
he ponders upon them.

The experiences of this day can be read on many different
levels—in one sense they are an initiation through which

man attains the power of living thinking; in another, the stages of experience between death and a new birth; or again, these epochs themselves. It seems simplest to follow the process as that of reincarnation and of the creation of a new resurrection body, the body that has been spoken of as the future gift of Christ to man. It should be noted that in the fifteenth century the understanding of reincarnation and karma was confined to those Rosicrucians who had attained to the highest degree of initiation. They placed this story before the world so that men might grow familiar with a picture which in the future could awaken within them an understanding of its full meaning. In the same way a real fairy tale conveys to a child in pictures spiritual wisdom which is only transformed into concepts much later in life.

The day begins with the old Warden's bestowal upon each guest of one of three means of climbing to the next higher stage of spiritual experience—wings, ladders and ropes. We note that they are given out by lot, and we remember how Christian Rosenkreutz was led, seemingly by chance, to one of the four roads that was his destined way. At crucial moments we may trust 'chance' events to be a surer guide to a right destiny than the conscious choice of the limited wisdom of man. 'Wings' are obviously the privilege of the very few initiates present, who can at will mount to each next higher realm. A 'ladder' is the picture of the means by which the spiritual seeker ascends who still rises step by step, not without effort, but in his own strength. Those who have 'ropes', whose spiritual exercises sit more lightly upon them day by day, find the climb more arduous and have to be helped by those above them.

The collaborators are first asked to pray for the success of their enterprises; it has been said that the scientist of the future will go to his laboratory table as to an altar. Now a great oval casket containing the bodies of the dead kings and queens is brought in, and also a small shrine containing the Moor's head. A fountain whose water is to be heated reminds us of the processes carried out in the alchemist's laboratory. The distillation is brought about to the strains of beautiful music. Of this Rudolf Steiner says: 'What the intellect perceives as *law*, in the spiritual world is *music*; all pictures shining with *light* are at the same time *sounding*.'

The tinctures and essences prepared the previous day, together with the Moor's head, are used in this first process. These, since the basis of matter and earthly substance is spirit, can generate the spiritual power and spiritual heat necessary to transform physical substance into etheric liquid. We remember the same process going on in the domain of a sleeping Venus. The liquid is then placed in a golden globe—gold is always an alchemical picture of the Sun Sphere, the Sphere of Christ.

Before each of the processes there is a creative pause of 'a quarter of an hour'. We notice that at each stage a preparation is made by an unseen being before the collaborators can begin their work. We realize the old Warden is active behind the scenes, though he is not seen, and then only by the chosen four, till the very end.

In this third storey they are in the Sun Sphere—there is sunlight everywhere, and it is the light and heat from the sun that creates the snow-white egg. We are made to realize something of the joy of creation—the guests 'are as jocund as if they themselves had laid the egg.' We are all too apt to think that any creative work in which we take a part is our own instead of realizing that we are, after all, only humble collaborators with the spiritual power that wills to work through and with us.

On the fourth floor, they see the Bird—the human soul in its astral condition—emerge; at first very wild, and only gradually tamed. Fed first on the essence of the former earth-life—the blood of the kings and queens—he grows feathers, always a picture of thoughts; memories of earth-life produce black feathers, unenlightened by heaven's wisdom. When a change is made to heavenly food the Bird's feathers become white. Later they are still further irradiated by the glory of heaven and become many-coloured and full of beauty. And now the Bird is docile and friendly.

In the fifth stage the Bird loses these transformed thoughts; in the alchemical process they become a blue liquid with which the Bird is painted, all except the head.

Blue is the colour of Saturn, the bearer of cosmic memory, who retains the essence of earthly thoughts which become deeds in a new life; for what has been learned in one life is transmuted into a faculty in the next. The head of one incarnation is, however, discarded; having served its purpose it is not painted with the rest of the body, and presently is struck off.

In the sixth storey we again find an altar. Previously, the altar showed man's relation to the cosmos from an earthly point of view; now it is seen from the cosmic aspect. The six objects had relation to the planets' work upon the earth; now we are shown that the planetary influence is powerful in forming the faculties of the human being in his new life. The collaborators make the Bird drink from the fountain of birth, to which he is averse—he pecks at the serpent till she bleeds, perhaps indicating the soul's reluctance to come into connexion with the mysteries of death and of rebirth. As Novalis has said, 'A birth on earth is a death in the spiritual worlds.'

The clock chimes when certain conjunctions are reached. It is the solemn 'midnight hour' when the soul must turn anew towards the earth. The hour of re-birth depends upon the constellation in the heavens—the soul's gifts and faculties must enter the world on the stream with which it is associated.[19] This does not mean that man is ruled by the stars, as the ancients thought, but reveals that a man, his fellow men, and the universe are one, and must live in mutual harmony.

The Bird's head is severed from the body; the forces of trunk and limbs will be transformed in the new life. This is the moment of sacrifice; the past is sacrificed that its forces may be metamorphosed into new ones for the future. The body is burned, together with a little tablet hanging by—the previous earth-life's karmic record; the ashes of both are preserved and used in the creation of the new body. The ashes represent the essence of the destiny of the soul, which is built into the whole structure of the human being about to be born.

And now Andreæ tells us of a little joke which the Virgin plays upon four of the wedding guests. (It is refreshing to

find that jokes are played in heaven.) Here Andreæ
deliberately keeps a light, satiric touch, to avoid any
approach to sentimentality. The Virgin pretends that
Christian Rosenkreutz, his friend, and two others have been
unsatisfactory co-workers; they are therefore not to take
part in the seventh process. Feeling very shame-faced, they
are driven from the room, only to find themselves led up
in honour to the eighth floor, and there met by the old
Warden, with whom they are now permitted to take part
in the final mystery of the new creation.[20]

The ashes are mixed with prepared water—the substance
of karma with the etheric life-forces—to shape the
transformed bodies of the young king and queen, which
at first are very tiny. While waiting to carry out the next
stage, the four guests watch the other five on the floor
below, busy carrying out alchemistic processes in the old
way, thinking that they are more honoured in this task than
the four who have left them. One imagines these could well
be the guests who in the Castle painted copies of the
beautiful pictures; they are not aware that something new
is needed at this momentous point in time.

The chosen four watch the little embryo forms grow and
are enchanted by their beauty. We feel again that here is
the joy of creation, known to all artists, and realize the truth
of Rudolf Steiner's words: 'Now there is nothing which may
in reality be called bliss except the vision of the process of
creation, the process of becoming.'

The tiny beings are fed with the Bird's blood, the
quintessence, it would seem, of the earlier life. They are
almost transparent—this is the fundamental form of the
resurrection body, which is to receive the soul. The old
Warden is active in this part of the initiation, 'performing
many ceremonial gestures towards the roof' where, as Christian Rosenkreutz knows, the souls are awaiting incarnation.
The trumpets are the means by which the souls enter the
mouths of the king and queen. They shoot down like a
brilliant streak of flame, and the images begin to stir. We
are reminded of the statue scene in Shakespeare's *The
Winter's Tale*, which is apparently written out of a
knowledge of this whole ceremony.

After a 'creative pause' during which the king and queen sleep, they are awakened and have no memory of anything that has happened to them since their last earth-life. At this point of time, man has no memory of the time between death and re-birth. The Virgin now clothes them in white garments 'which could have been crystal but that they are gentle and not transparent'—a beautiful description of the new fleshly body. They now start on their journey to the scene of their earthly activities.

The nine guests meet again at supper which is made into a festival by the wisdom and charm of the old Warden, the Lord of Olympus. Afterwards they are shown the rarities in the Tower. We remember that we are in the region of archetypes, the realm of Jupiter.

At length they sleep. Their work of transubstantiation is complete. Rudolf Steiner reminds us that such a process is not carried out solely for the benefit of the individuality concerned, but for humanity. Later on there must be brought about, by already transformed individualities, the transubstantiation of *society*; and later again that transubstantiation of *the earth* of which St Paul speaks.

The Seventh Day (Friday)

After their wonderful experience in the heights, the guests are led back to the lowest regions of the Tower, preparatory to their return to earth-life. They now wear yellow garments (the colour of Mercury), together with the insignia of the Golden Fleece.

The old lord, the Warden, gives each a medallion. On the one side is inscribed 'Art is the priestess of Nature.' The process which they have just carried out is 'art' in the deepest sense of the word. By penetrating to the realm where Nature weaves the dead into the living and becoming, they have carried this process further in the transubstantiation of the being of man. The other side of the medallion bears the words, 'Nature is the Daughter of Time.' Evolution gradually comes forth from the womb of time. Although the events of the previous day have only been briefly portrayed, the seven storeys of the Tower remind us of the time-element which must be present in all growth and becoming.

The guests re-cross the sea in ships that now bear, not the planetary signs, but the signs of the zodiac. They sail under Libra—the sign of balance; they are still in 'the year of balance' and, moreover, have now to find the balance between spiritual and temporal existence. Christian Rosenkreutz is especially delighted by the company of the old lord: 'I could have sailed with him all my life long.' We remember his comment on the previous day: 'If men would but take notice of his procedure things would not so often and so untowardly miscarry.' We are given a glimpse of what it can mean to men to develop the power to make contact in full consciousness with great earthly personalities who are living in the spiritual world, and take council with them. Rudolf Steiner has spoken of the importance of developing the power to bring about this conscious inter-weaving between the two worlds. In *Some Characteristics of Today*, he has said: 'This is the sole real healing that humanity needs.'

We shall now return to the level of interpretation which portrays Christian Rosenkreutz as having experienced an initiation through which his higher self has been brought to birth within him.

The travellers are greeted by five hundred ships which come out to meet them—perhaps (like the parable of the five thousand) an indication of the Fifth Post-Atlantean Age in which we are living. Old Atlas (the earth-bearer) comes forth eagerly to greet them, for 'the earth is hungry for initiates.' [21]

The other five guests are astonished to see the young king, already alive and active. The four who took part in the final awakening are silent as to this; the initiate's lips are sealed concerning his most inward experiences.

The old lord gives his warm good wishes to the young couple and then delivers into the hands of Cupid a small casket, the contents of which are kept secret. [22]

The shore where they land is near the first gate at which Christian Rosenkreutz had entered. The initiate has to return

to his earth-life precisely at the point where he stood before
his initiation. The young king, the old lord and himself are
now given horses—they have now to resume earthly thinking. They carry a snow-white ensign with a red cross; this,
the ensign carried by the Risen Christ, was also the flag both
of St George and of the Templars. In response to the young
king's question, he tells him how he gave up his water and
salt (personal feeling and thinking) in return for the token
on his cap. The young king then tells him he is *his* father—
the initiate may in a sense be said to have fathered the birth
of his own higher self.

And now we are told of a very strange happening in which
Christian Rosenkreutz becomes the Guardian of the modern
age, replacing the former Guardian. This he at first regards
as a punishment, not understanding its full significance. The
old Guardian delivers to him a petition for the king, begging to be relieved of his task. He also had 'looked upon
Venus' and had been condemned to be gate-keeper until
another committed the same fault.

In earlier times it was not permitted even in initiation to
enter consciously the realm where life is generated. Procreation took place in unconscious sleep. But in the new
initiation it is permissible, and indeed necessary, to enter
this dangerous realm. Christian Rosenkreutz does not, however, realize that he is guiltless, and therefore suffers
torments of conscience. It seems that the young king and
the old lord are in no haste to reassure him. One has a feeling
that this portrays the way in which the working of the
spiritual world is often misunderstood by the human being.
As the old lord had remarked on the previous day, 'Man
never knoweth how well God intendeth him.' The Rosicrucian Brother has to take his courage in both hands to
make a full confession, saying that as the old gatekeeper
had been his benefactor on his arrival at the castle, he must
set him free at whatever cost to himself. He feels he must
repay his debt to ancient wisdom, which has been the foundation on which his new knowledge has grown. He sadly
receives the ring of office thinking that he must for many
years 'sit under his gate.'

He is becoming the gatekeeper, also, of his own thoughts

and inner life, and this does not, as he fears, preclude him from entering the spiritual world but is in fact a necessity. He is also to work for humanity, and this is shown by his being made, together with the other guests, 'Knight of the Golden Stone.' To see dead substance as a revelation of the spirit, this is the Golden Stone. Ordinary knowledge is a corpse; spirit-permeated knowledge is the Golden Stone. But also the spirit-permeated body is the Golden Stone. And Knights of the Golden Stone are those who, having brought about this transubstantiation in themselves and in their thinking, are pledged to work for the transubstantiation of society, as indicated by the five vows.

That the initiate's new work for humanity will not be allowed to unfold unhampered by the Spirits of Hindrance has already been pictured forth in the game 'not unlike chess', with the virtues and vices pitted one against the other, played by the young king and queen. It warns the spiritual seeker that to range oneself on the side of the Spirits of Light is to invite attacks from the Spirits of Darkness. It is interesting to recall that one of Dr Steiner's exhortations to vigilance in face of such surprise attacks on the part of the Adversary is couched in terms of this particular Imagination: 'Never forget the Invisible Chess-Player.'

At the end of this troublous day Christian Rosenkreutz finds himself, greatly to his surprise, honoured by sleeping with the old lord and Atlas. Again and again we see in him this quality of beautiful humility, which is always startled to find a recognition of any spiritual stature in himself.

Abruptly he 'came home' into the physical body. Even if he is the 'Guardian' of the Age, the spiritual seeker of today must re-enter everyday life, and continue earthly tasks; but now his higher self is working in all that he does. The young king had said, 'This is the last time you will see me *in this manner*', which our friend had taken to be a farewell. But though it is only in the spiritual world that we can see the higher self face to face, as it were, this higher self, once won, works on within us. We do not behold, but we feel, its power.

Rudolf Steiner concludes his comments by saying: 'Doubtless some readers will be specially curious to know how the change was accomplished, but only one who has experienced it can understand the transition back to everyday life. Andreæ says, "one or two pages are lost" thus showing how expertly he understands the conditions of esoteric life.'

Part Three

Notes

1. Rudolf Steiner, Lecture, 9 December, 1923 (*Mystery Knowledge and Mystery Centres*).
2. Andreæ calls 1459 'a year of balance' and it is important to understand why. We know that the laws of cause and effect work in such a way that the cause of a certain happening may be sought the same number of years before the 'point of balance' as the event happened after. Thus, if we take away 1459 from 1604, when the story was written down, we arrive at a period of 145 years. Now, 145 years before 1459, in 1314, the Order of the Knights Templar was suppressed by Philippe le Bel. The Rosicrucian Order had the task of carrying forward the work of this Order.

   Moreover, the year 1459 may be called 'a year of balance' in a much deeper sense. Rudolf Steiner has called the year AD 333 the dead centre of earth-evolution. Owing to a time-lag caused by the Spirits of Hindrance, the second half of earth evolution actually began in 1413, at the dawn of the fifth cultural epoch, its workings being first actively implemented in 1459 by the founding of the Rosicrucian Order.

   This may also be spoken of as the transition from the Mars half to the Mercury half of earth-evolution; during the first half, the Mars-forces of materialization were working; during the second half the Mercury-forces, etherealizing matter, must increasingly hold sway. Thus the Mars half of the earth's history has meant the growth of intellectual thinking, and ever deeper descent into materialism, while the Mercury half will bring the development of living thinking. The Mars-period has brought about a hardening of man's physical body; the Mercury-period brings the possibility of its etherization. We may refer here to Rudolf Steiner's *The Theosophy of the Rosicrucians* and *At the Gates of Spiritual Science*.

   There is yet another important respect in regard to which this was a time of balance. A danger had arisen that mankind would split into two groups, those who wished to live a spiritual life in seclusion and those who carried out the practical life of the world. A form of intitiation had to be instituted which would not preclude the spiritual seeker from taking part in the life of the everyday world. Christian Rosenkreutz was the first of the new initiates whose task it was, and is, to find the balance between spiritual and material life.

3. It is important to know, concerning an individuality, not only who he was, but also to which stream of humanity he belongs. This is of especial import in the case of Christian Rosenkreutz. He is the Guardian of the modern age of technology; as such he belongs to the Cain-Hiram stream. This is made clear through the Temple Legend, entrusted by Christian Rosenkreutz to the Brotherhood of the Rose Cross.

In this we are told that Cain was the son of Eve and one of the Elohim, while Jahve created Adam, whose sons by Eve were Abel and Seth. Jahve accepted the offering of Abel, but rejected that of Cain, because the latter had not been created at His command. Cain therefore slew Abel and was cast out from the company of Jahve.

From the race of Cain came all that had to do with the earth; he and his descendants originated Art and Science. One of his descendants, Tubal-Cain, was skilled in the handling and mixing of metals. From this same line came Hiram, the famous Master Builder, skilled in all the science and technology of his age.

Solomon was descended from the race of Seth, gifted in all that Jahve could bestow of tranquil wisdom. He conceived the magnificent idea and plan of the Temple, but his wisdom had nothing to do with technology or the creations of the human will; therefore he had to call in Hiram to aid him. The divine wisdom of Solomon was to be the heart of the Temple, clothed in earthly substance by the skill of Hiram.

But at this time Balkis, Queen of Sheba, bearer of the old clairvoyance, visted Solomon and was wooed by him. Having accepted the king, she met Hiram and

straightway fell in love with him, thereby rousing bitter jealously in her royal lover. Solomon's enmity
brought about Hiram's death.

From this time on, the two streams, Cain-Hiram,
Abel-Seth-Solomon, pursued their way through the
centuries, the rift unhealed; the sons of Cain still
masters of art and science, the sons of Solomon pursuing philosophy and religion. It was the task of Christian Rosenkreutz to unite both streams in his own
being and thus begin the healing of the breach.

4. Our present era, the era in which man was to develop
the Consciousness Soul, began in 1413. In the evolution of the single individuality, the Consciousness
Soul is developed in the seven years from thirty-five
to forty-two.

Christian Rosenkreutz was thirty-five in 1413—a
further instance of the wonderful way in which his
own evolution harmonized with world-evolution.

Incidentally it may be noted here that as one aspect
of the Consciousness Soul man develops the 'onlooker
consciousness', and with regard to the experiences
about to be related, Christian Rosenkreutz is at once
participator and onlooker.

5. *Fama Fraternitatis Roseæ Crucis* (first printed 1614).

6. Rudolf Steiner, *The Problems of Our Time*.

7. Christian Rosenkreutz is careful to show that his
adventure begins on Easter Eve, Saturday. It is important to notice that each succeeding day has a character
of its own, corresponding to its planetary significance.
We recall that Saturday is Saturn's day, a day dedicated
to reviewing the past, for Saturn is the bearer of
cosmic memory; it is therefore the appropriate day
for Christian Rosenkreutz to review his own past
before deciding whether he is worthy to undertake
the journey. Saturn is also the planet of destiny, and
today is a fateful day for him.

Sunday belongs to the Sun and is a day of new begin-
nings. On this day he sets out on a journey which may
be said to be a new beginning not only for himself
but for all humanity.

Monday, the Moon's day, reminds us that this cosmic body possesses great hardening forces and promotes a tendency towards materialism, but also towards atavistic clairvoyance. These must be consciously resisted and overcome if a man is to be a true spiritual seeker. Hence, in the story, Monday is the day of testing the guests.

Tuesday (in Old Germanic, Ziu's day, in French *mardi*) is the day of Mars. Wednesday (in Germanic, Wotan's day, in French, *mercredi*) is the day of Mercury. In the story, Tuesday, the day of 'dying into matter', is the day the kings are beheaded. Wednesday (Mercury's day) sees the beginning of the process of resurrection.

Thursday (in Germanic, Thor's day, in French, *jeudi*) is Jove's or Jupiter's day. The planet Jupiter is the realm of archetypes, of Plato's Ideas. It is fitting that on this day the guests are at work in the Tower of Jupiter bringing to consummation the resurrection of the kings. In the next incarnation of the earth, called the Jupiter-evolution, man himself will be called upon to take a hand in creation.

Friday (in Germanic, Freya's day, in French, *vendredi*) is the day of Venus. The true Venus holds the mystery of selfless love and service of our fellow men. On this day the guests are made Knights of the Golden Stone.

We can understand this amazing narrative in many ways—as the story of an initiation, leading to living thinking; as the story of man's evolution, leading to his developing the 'resurrection body'; as a picture of human development throughout the seven culture epochs of earth evolution; and, again, as a picture of the seven incarnations of the earth. And in the names of the consecutive days of the week, we have reminders of all these stages of development.

8. The wound in the head: Christian Rosenkreutz here hints at the mysterious connexion that exists between ideation and procreation. In times long past, when the sexes were first divided, conscious spiritual activity

began. From that moment part of the energy which man had hitherto used in bringing forth children was directed towards the development of his own being. The power with which man has been enabled to create for himself an instrument of thought is the very same power whereby in very ancient times he fertilized himself. Thus we discover from Rudolf Steiner's lecture, 'Atlantis and Lemuria'.

This gives a key to the temptation that assails the highly intellectual man, and explains the connexion twice spoken of by Christian Rosenkreutz between the 'wound in the head' and his meeting with Venus, also his reaction to the song of the sirens. It is interesting that the genius of language retains an awareness of this connexion in that the same word, fertilization, may refer to an idea, a conception in the mind, as well as to procreation, the conceiving of a new human being.

9. The roses are a picture of the development of the so-called lotus-flowers, the organs of higher perception: the two-petalled between the eyes, the sixteen-petalled in the larynx, the twelve-petalled in the region of the heart and the ten-petalled at the pit of the stomach. These are the first four to be developed. Rudolf Steiner's *Knowledge of the Higher Worlds* may be referred to here. It is interesting that the first Rosicrucian cross was pictured with four roses; the others were added later.

10. The Resurrection Body: In the lectures, *From Jesus to Christ*, Dr Steiner devotes much time and thought to this all-important subject. Briefly, he says: What is the physical body? We are accustomed to say that man lays aside his physical body at death. But is this really so? What man puts off at death no longer possesses the most important thing that his body has in life—namely, its form. In a short time it crumbles into formless earthly substances. It is quite clear, then, that the *form*, which is the real physical body, withdraws at death. To the substances and forces which a man has experienced as his physical body

during life, something else has been added, the *form*, or as Dr Steiner calls it, the *phantom*. In the earliest days of man's incarnation, the physical body was not visible. It only became visible after the Fall, when Lucifer led men more and more deeply into physical matter, which was necessary if man was to win the gift of freedom. The physical body is really transparent, crystal clear. Through Lucifer men have taken earth substances and forces into this body—it has become solid and opaque, and at the same time it has taken into itself the forces of death. By the time of the Mystery of Golgotha there was a danger that the body would become unfit as a vehicle for the ego of man.

Then came the Mystery of Golgotha, and through this happening it came to pass that one man, who was the bearer of the Christ, passed through such a death that after three days the specifically mortal part disappeared into the earth, and from the grave there arose the pure phantom—that which it was intended from the beginning man should have. The spiritual body which rose from death on the first Easter gradually imparts itself to every man who makes the right connexion with Christ. In the future this body will be the gift of Christ to every man who has chosen to take His forces into himself.

Dr Zeylmans van Emmichoven points out, in *The Foundation Stone*, that the true purpose of the true alchemist was to prepare this higher body. We shall see on the sixth day how Christian Rosenkreutz does this.

11. *Occult Science* tells us that the four roads are the paths opened up by the four incarnations of our planet— the Old Saturn, Old Sun, Old Moon and Earth evolutions.

The rocky and dangerous road is that of Ancient Moon; the long, safe road, that of Earth; the Royal Road, that of Ancient Sun, which only high initiates may travel; the road 'fit only for incorruptible bodies' is the way of Old Saturn.

At this point a tentative hypothesis may be put forward. We learn from Rudolf Steiner's *The East in the Light of the West* that in the fourth century the great Manes called together in the supersensible world the three great Bodhisattvas, Scythianos, Buddha and Zazrathustra, and that at this Council a plan for the future evolution of the civilizations of the Earth was decided upon and carried over into the European Mysteries of the Rose Cross. As the *Chymical Wedding* in 1459 was the inception of their plan for the modern age, it would seem natural to suppose that these three exalted individualities were present among the wedding guests: Scythianos, as the Initiate of the West, travelling, but immaculately, by the rocky road; Zarathustra, as a King of Wisdom, by the Royal Road; and the Buddha by the Saturn Road, 'fit only for incorruptible bodies'; and that in the Initiator directing the alchemical processes of re-birth the great Manes himself could be indicated.

12. There is only one individuality of whom Rudolf Steiner has said that he was the friend (and pupil) of Christain Rosenkreutz (see *The Mission of Christian Rosenkreutz*) and that is the Buddha, whom he sent to Mars in 1604, the year in which *The Chymical Wedding* was written down. Supposing the Buddha to have been among the guests, would it not be likeliest that it is he who is 'the fine, quiet man' whom our traveller henceforth refers to as his friend and companion?

13. Rudolf Steiner, *Karmic Relationships Vol. 3*.

14. It has been suggested that the first Emperor may be thought of as Solomon, a man rich in all wisdom, which he possessed as a gift from above with no effort on his own part. He had a wealth of star-wisdom, but it was not till much later that man began to explore the depths of his own soul, and to strive to unite it with the cosmos. We know from Steiner's *The Reappearance of Christ in the Etheric* that the wisdom of the Solomonic Age was repeated in the first millennium after Christ, and that the spirit of Solomon

lived and moved in the most outstanding figures of that age. But it was not until towards the close of the first thousand years after Christ that men attained any degree of *self*-consciousness. We remember that Astronomica, as taught in later centuries, revealed how through a knowledge of the planets the pupils could learn the secrets of the soul, and through an apprehension of the zodiac the secrets of the ego. This knowledge Solomon could not attain in earlier days. May it not be that for this reason he cannot sustain the seventh weight? Yet, having such riches of cosmic wisdom, the failure would be very bitter to him. If this is a true reading of the story, it is easy to understand that Christian Rosenkreutz might take the opportunity of a gesture towards healing the age-long breach between the two streams here represented. Unhappily, we see that the Emperor does not respond to this overture of friendship.

It has been surmised that the only Emperor to pass the test, described as 'a short man with a curly brown beard', might be Zarathustra, pictured as he may well have appeared as Zarathos, in Babylon, in the sixth century BC. It will not seem so surprising that this wisest of men does not far surpass the other guests if we remember that already as Zarathos his teaching was a mere shadow of Zarathustra's radiant wisdom because of the density of the body then available—a handicap which had grown even more serious by the time of the *Chymical Wedding*.

15. Another possible confirmation of the conjecture concerning the Buddha (described by Dr Steiner as the friend and pupil of Christian Rosenkreutz) is the fact that it is the latter's page—*his* initiative—who leads *both* in their exploration of the Castle.

16. Fully to understand this experience we must recall a further incident in the Temple Legend.

Hiram wanted to mingle the seven metals in a Brazen Sea as the climax of his achievement in the construction of the Temple. Some jealous apprentices spoilt his work by pouring water in a wrong way into the molten metal. Hiram, in despair, heard the voice of his ancestor, Tubal-Cain, telling him to plunge fearlessly into the sea of molten metal through which he would come to the centre of the earth and there learn the secret of rightly uniting fire and water, that is, the secret of rightly uniting water with the seven molten metals.

This is the innermost secret of the Rosicrucians: how to mingle the fire of enthusiasm with the water of calm wisdom. It is the uniting of the Cain and Abel streams, the Hiram and Solomon streams, which will only gradually emerge into the reality of the physical world. It is brought about by the activity of the stars *within* the earth, portrayed in the seven metals of the Brazen Sea. It is the contemplation of this planetary activity while they are sitting at the centre of the great globe that so deeply absorbs the two friends.

17. For further understanding of the principle of metamorphosis see Goethe's *The Metamorphosis of Plants* or the explanation of Goethe's work in *Man or Matter* by Ernst Lehrs.

18. See 'The First Goetheanum as a Modern Mystery Temple' by D. J. van Bemmelen (*Anthroposophical Quarterly*, Spring 1964).

19. See Rudolf Steiner, *Between Death and Rebirth*.

20. The reader is referred back to Note 11, in which the spiritual Council of the fourth century is mentioned. The crucial event now to be described is the first unfolding of the plan then decided upon. We may therefore form a hypothesis that the 'Old Warden' is none other than Manes. He is active behind the scenes until the last process is reached and then is seen only by the chosen four, who are allowed to collaborate with him in the highest and most occult process in the eighth storey.

The creation of the resurrection body takes place in the Tower of Olympus, the region of Jupiter. On the planet Jupiter a colony of advanced spiritual beings is working at the preparation of the future Jupiter condition of the Earth. The stream of Christian

Rosenkreutz co-operates with them in this preparation, of which the alchemical processes taking place in the Tower of Olympus are in a certain sense a part. Dr Steiner tells us, in *The Mission of Folk-Souls*, that these Spirits of Jupiter were specially observed in that fourth century Council, when Scythianos, Zarathustra and Buddha, under the guidance of Manes, met to investigate the forces which must be developed for the evolution of humanity from a starting point connected with the Jupiter forces—that is, to develop Imagination, Inspiration and Intuition through the senses and the sense world.

21. In *The Portal of Initiation*, Felix Balde, the nature mystic, comes to the Temple of Hidden Wisdom with this message:

> A power which speaks from very depths
>   of earth
> Unto my spirit, hath commanded me
> To come unto this consecrated place;
> Since it desires to speak to you through
>   me
> Of all its bitter sorrow and its need.

22. It is possible that the contents of the casket delivered over to the care of Cupid, which cannot then be revealed, are concerned with the procreation of the future, when Venus will awake and appear in her real being.

Concerning this secret, Rudolf Steiner says, in *The Theosophy of the Rosicrucians*, that the generative process and all that stands in connexion with it will in the future pass over to another organ. The organ that is already preparing to be the future organ of generation is the human larynx. Later on, not only will the word be spoken forth by the larynx, but man will pour forth his forces into the word in such a way that he will 'speak forth' a new human being, his own likeness. This in the future will be the birth of a new man—that he is spoken forth by another.

Bibliography

Abbreviations used in the bibliography

RSP   Rudolf Steiner Press, London
AP   Anthroposophic Press, New York
RSPC Rudolf Steiner Publishing Co., London
APC   Anthroposophical Publishing Co., London

Translations of the text

Johann Valentine Andreæ, *The Chymical Wedding of Christian Rosenkreutz Anno 1459*, Minerva Books, distributed by RSP. (Translated from the High Dutch by Edward Foxcroft in 1690.)

Johann Valentine Andreæ and Jon Valentine, *The Chymical Wedding of Christian Rosenkreutz Anno 1459*, St George Publications, New York, 1981. (A modern poetic version by Jon Valentine with illustrations by Arne Salomonsen.)

Works referred to in the text and other relevant works

Paul M. Allen, *A Christian Rosenkreutz Anthology*, Rudolf Steiner Publications, New York, 1974.

D.J. van Bemmelen, 'The First Goetheanum as a Modern Mystery Temple', *Anthroposophical Quarterly*, 9, 1, Spring 1964.

Dr. F.W. Zeylmans van Emmichoven, *The Foundation Stone*, RSP, 1963.

Fama Fraternitatis Rosae Crucis, (Kassel, 1916), also published in Paul M. Allen, *A Christian Rosenkreutz Anthology*.

J.W. von Goethe, *The Metamorphosis of Plants*, Biodynamic Literature, 1974.

Ernst Lehrs, *Man or Matter*, RSP, 1985.

Hinricus Madathanus Theosophus, *Secret Symbols of the Rosicrucians*, (German title: *Die geheimen Figuren der Rosenkreutzer*, Altona, 1785/88).

Rudolf Steiner, *Atlantis and Lemuria*, APC, 1923.

Rudolf Steiner, *At the Gates of Spiritual Science*, RSP, 1986.

Rudolf Steiner, *Between Death and Rebirth*, RSP, 1975.

Rudolf Steiner, 'The Chymical Wedding of Christian Rosenkreutz', (*Das Reich*, Oct 1917-April 1918), published in Paul M. Allen, *A Christian Rosenkreutz Anthology*.

Rudolf Steiner, *The East in the Light of the West*, AP, 1940.

Rudolf Steiner, 'The European Mysteries and their Initiates', lecture given in 1909, *Anthroposophical Quarterly*, 9, 1, Spring 1964.

Rudolf Steiner, *From Jesus to Christ*, RSP, 1973.

Rudolf Steiner, *Karmic Relationships Vol. 3*, RSP, 1977.

Rudolf Steiner, *Knowledge of the Higher Worlds*, RSP, 1976.

Rudolf Steiner, *The Mission of Christian Rosenkreutz: its Character and Purpose*. See *Esoteric Christianity and the Mission of Christian Rosenkreutz*, RSP, 1984.

Rudolf Steiner, *The Mission of Folk-Souls*, RSP, 1970.

Rudolf Steiner, *Mystery Knowledge and Mystery Centres*, RSP, 1973.

Rudolf Steiner, *Occult Science*, RSP, 1969.

Rudolf Steiner, 'The Portal of Initiation', in *Four Mystery Plays*, RSP, 1976.

Rudolf Steiner, *Planetary Spheres and their Influence on Man's Life on Earth and in the Spiritual Worlds*, RSP, 1982.

Rudolf Steiner, *The Problems of our Time*, AP, 1943.

Rudolf Steiner, *The Reappearance of Christ in the Etheric*, AP, 1983.

Rudolf Steiner, *Rosicrucianism and Modern Initiation*, RSP, 1962.

Rudolf Steiner, *Some Characteristics of Today*, H. Collison, London, 1932.

Rudolf Steiner, *The Temple Legend*, RSP, 1985.

Rudolf Steiner, *The Theosophy of the Rosicrucians*, RSP, 1966.

The Twelve Holy Nights and the Spiritual Hierarchies

Sergei O. Prokofieff

This work is an important contribution to the new Cosmic Christianity of the twentieth century. It shows the relationship between the Hierarchies, the zodiac, and the earthly world. It includes a study of the working of the Hierarchies over time during the twelve Holy Nights, the first Goetheanum (Rudolf Steiner's portrayal of cosmic forces in earthly space), and the relationship between the zodiac, the first Goetheanum and the inner development of the human being. We now have to build the first Goetheanum in oursleves and, through the schooling of the etheric, strive for a twentieth century way of initiation.

The book is published 1000 years after the founding of Christianity in Russia. It offers an approach to star-wisdom which is Michaelic: free of speculative claims, in tune with present-day consciousness, universal, with hope for the future, spiritual yet down to earth.

Published 1988

Available from

TEMPLE
LODGE
PRESS

REINCARNATION WITHIN CHRISTIANITY

Evelyn Francis Capel

This book is an introduction to the study of reincarnation. It is intended to provoke thought and to stimulate further study of the subject. It is concerned with questions that the individual may have about reincarnation. It also looks at reincarnation in a broader historical context. Why has the idea of reincarnation been missing in the Western world for so long? What about reincarnation and Christianity?

The author shows that reincarnation can be accepted as a meaningful concept within Christian thought. Various episodes from the Old and New Testaments are examined from this point of view. Indeed it is her conviction that we can think afresh about Christianity if we approach it with a modern way of thinking.

Published 1988

Available from

DEATH

Evelyn Francis Capel

Death, 'the great reaper', confronts us all. Illness and bereavement challenge us, perhaps beyond our capacity. How can we meet these inexorable human dramas with understanding? Drawing on the work of Rudolf Steiner, Evelyn Capel argues that death is a stage in the spiritual development of the individual. Fear, caring, mourning, the death of a child, the book ranges widely and will enlighten and reassure all who are genuinely concerned to explore this mysterious area.

Published 1987

Available from

THE NINTH CENTURY AND THE HOLY GRAIL

Walter Johannes Stein

The ninth century is almost completely ignored in our historical education. Perhaps a brief mention of the Dark Ages—but little else. According to the author of this book it was a time of decisive and far-reaching inner and outer events, which have influenced the course of history to the present day. Taking his cue from personal conversations with Rudolf Steiner in 1923, Dr Stein places these events in their historical and spiritual context, and includes a detailed study of *Parzival*, Wolfram von Eschenbach's epic medieval poem: one of the great works of world literature.

Parzival's quest for the Holy Grail emerges as an archetype for human striving in the present age, and raises many questions concerning the moral life. It is easy to make speculative and wild claims about the story of the Holy Grail. Dr Stein's book adopts a scholarly approach which is, at the same time, inspiring.

Published 1988

Available from

TEMPLE
LODGE
PRESS